50 *Years of*
HOPE

Hi Jim,
1-26-2014
It was a pleasure getting
this book for you. I know you
will enjoy it. It's been great
working for you at the Farmers
Insurance open at Torrey Pines.
Best of luck to you.

Open AFB lunch
Navae Driver Marshal

To Jim,
"Hope" you enjoy the book!!
Larry Bohannan

Published by Pediment Publishing, a division of The Pediment Group, Inc. www.pediment.com Printed in Canada

Prologue

October, 2009

Dear Collector,

You are about to take a trip down memory lane – a "THANKS FOR THE MEMORY" trip.

As you turn these pages, you will be taken through fifty years of the BOB HOPE CLASSIC, one of the longest running Pro-Am golf tournaments on the PGA TOUR.

The names, the faces and the stories of your favorite pros, celebrities and amateurs will be vividly recalled to your memory.

The "trip" begins with the very first Classic played in 1960, won by Arnold Palmer, and goes through the 50th anniversary tournament played in 2009 and hosted by that same iconic Arnold Palmer.

During those fifty years, the CLASSIC has contributed over $47 million to the Eisenhower Medical Center and over 100 other deserving charities, all in the Coachella Valley.

Without you, our loyal fans, the cooperation of great sponsors and the tireless efforts of the thousands of volunteers who gave so much of their time through the years, this never would have happened.

We look forward to continuing this "trip" for the next fifty years and hope you will join us.

Sincerely,

Ernie Dunlevie
Founding Member,
Chairman of the Board, and
President Emeritus

Foreword

Dear Golf Enthusiasts:

For 50 years, the Bob Hope Classic has played a fabled role in our Coachella Valley and around the world. Since its February 1960 debut, few PGA tournaments have matched its star power, drama and prestige. For our community, the classic has pumped millions of dollars into countless charities. It is truly a sports and philanthropic gem of our Southern California desert. The Desert Sun is pleased to present, "50 Years of Hope," a celebration of the tournament, celebrities and charitable achievements of the Bob Hope Classic. Larry Bohannan, our staff golf reporter, has recounted the greatest moments of the event, providing a half-century analysis of the top players, biggest laughs and amazing civic contributions the tournament has provided. His behind-the-scenes story is set against the backdrop of one of the world's most iconic and beloved entertainers – Bob Hope, the cherished namesake of this event and the driving force behind its success. Now, tee up and relive the history, the Hollywood stars, the competition and the rich chapter that the Bob Hope Classic has played in our desert and the international golf scene.

Sincerely,

Richard A. Ramhoff
President and Publisher
The Desert Sun

Greg Castro
Marketing Director
The Desert Sun

Rick Green
Executive Editor
The Desert Sun

Table of Contents

Golf Among the Palms

·······································

*I*t was January 1959, and golf in Palm Springs was in trouble.

Oh, the recreational game was in fine shape in the Southern California desert. In just the previous decade, such fabled golf courses as Thunderbird, Tamarisk, Indian Wells, Eldorado, La Quinta and Bermuda Dunes had opened or were within months of debuting in the Palm Springs area.

The courses served a growing permanent population in the area. But they also were magnets, attracting new and part-time residents who discovered a golfing paradise in the desert dunes, the surrounding rugged mountains and the perfect winter weather of the Coachella Valley.

There was a reason why Palm Springs and the surrounding desert, in less than a decade, had blossomed into the self-proclaimed "Winter Golf Capital of the World."

No, in January 1959, it was the professional game that

ABOVE: The original club house at Thunderbird Country Club in Rancho Mirage, early 1950s.
Courtesy Rancho Mirage Public Library

was in danger of dying in the desert.

Palm Springs' stop on the winter swing of the professional golf tour, the Thunderbird Invitational, was screeching to an abrupt halt after the 1959 tournament. It debuted in 1952 as an unofficial tournament. The Thunderbird International was falling victim to three common problems plaguing tour events then and now:

• The purse, just $15,000, was too small even by 1959 standards.

• The Thunderbird course, designed as a winter haven for residents of such northern cities as Chicago and Seattle, was proving too easy for the talented pros.

• And some Thunderbird members, a mix of high-powered corporate presidents and some of the world's best-known entertainers, were weary of yielding their golf course for a week while other memberships were still free to play their courses.

The death of a tour event in the increasingly popular Coachella Valley, two hours east of Los Angeles, was unthinkable to local officials. It became the urgent subject of an impromptu meeting on the back of the Thunderbird driving range after a stunning come-from-behind victory in the event by Arnold Palmer.

Some of the biggest figures from the desert golf scene were part of the meeting: Milt Hicks, past president of Thunderbird, an original investor in Indian Wells Country Club and the chairman of two Ryder Cup matches in the Palm Springs area; Ernie Dunlevie, a long-time desert resident and co-developer of the new Bermuda Dunes Country Club course; Johnny Dawson, an accomplished amateur player whose vision transformed Thunderbird from a dude ranch into Palm Springs' first 18-hole golf course in 1951; and from Tamarisk Country Club, brothers Ed and Ellsworth Vines, the latter a two-time U.S. Open tennis champion who later became a golf professional.

That meeting gave birth to the Palm Springs Golf Classic, a world-renowned tournament that later became the Bob Hope Chrysler Classic.

For the next five decades, the tournament thrust Palm Springs into the global spotlight, solidifying its image as a playground for Hollywood stars, politicians and even presidents. It also branded the desert as a haven for golfers, helped build a world-class hospital and provided a glitzy stage for its namesake and the sport's best ambassador, Bob Hope.

The idea of the Coachella Valley without a professional tournament seemed absurd even in the 1950s.

The area had grown from just a handful of golf holes in the 1940s to a dozen 18-hole courses by that 1959 Thunderbird tournament. The desert even hosted the Ryder Cup matches, the biennial matches between teams from the U.S. and the combined squad of Great Britain and Ireland. Thunderbird had hosted the 1955 Ryder Cup, while Eldorado would host the 1959 matches.

The appeal of the area was plain as the nose on Hope's face, even if the California desert seemed one of the most unlikely spots in the world to become a golf mecca.

The Palm Springs area was full of sandy dunes, high winds and rugged, rocky mountains that seemed inhospitable for humans, much less golf courses.

BELOW: Thunderbird Dude Ranch in Rancho Mirage was developed in the mid-1940s, but with the addition of a golf course became Thunderbird Country Club in 1951.
Courtesy Rancho Mirage Public Library

9

But the sport took root here, thanks to perfect winter weather and an underground secret: a massive water aquifer beneath the barren desert landscape that gave green fairways and putting greens their brilliant color beneath the withering desert sun.

Still, golf's explosion in the desert came with a delayed fuse.

The first courses in the desert were built in the 1920s, including the Mashie Course at the famed Desert Inn in Palm Springs and nine holes at La Quinta Resort in La Quinta, some 20 miles by dirt road from downtown Palm Springs. While those courses would eventually die out, oilman Tom O'Donnell's nine-hole course in Palm Springs not only survived, but thrived.

Pros played the course from time to time, but O'Donnell's course became the popular spot for the Hollywood celebrities who were increasingly adopting the desert as a weekend getaway and winter residence. It wasn't uncommon to walk down to O'Donnell and see foursomes that included Danny Kaye, Jack Benny or even a Marx brother or two.

And, of course, there was always Bob Hope.

Bob and Dolores Hope had moved to California in 1937 as Bob was preparing to film his first movie, "The Big Broadcast of 1938." It was in that movie that Hope first crooned what would become his theme song – and eventually the anthem of his golf tournament – "Thanks for the Memories."

It didn't take long for the Hopes to discover the secret that many in Hollywood already knew. Palm Springs was a great place to get away for a weekend, especially if you wanted to sneak in a round of golf.

"We came down because we were golf nuts, and they were playing a golf tournament at O'Donnell," Dolores

Hope said. "That's a thousand years ago, of course. I'm old enough to remember before that. We stayed at the old El Mirador hotel, came down with two friends of ours and spent the weekend and fell madly in love with Palm Springs."

After that, the Hopes made trips to the desert resort as often as possible.

"We finally bought a little house in 1941, and we bought another little house in 1946," Mrs. Hope said.

Eventually, the Hopes would build perhaps the most famous house in the desert, a saucer-shaped home on a ridge in the mountains overlooking south Palm Springs.

O'Donnell and Cochran Ranch, a nine-hole course built in the 1940s in Indio by aviatrix Jackie Cochran and her husband, were popular courses with celebrities and the growing population of the Coachella Valley. But the true marriage of Hollywood, high-powered CEOs and golf pros began with the opening of Thunderbird Country Club.

Thunderbird was the vision of Johnny Dawson, an excellent amateur golfer who won three Trans-Mississippi titles, almost every amateur title available in California and even won Bing Crosby's pro-am tournament in 1942 at Rancho Santa Fe Country Club in San Diego. Five years later, he was runner-up in the 1947 U.S. Amateur at Pebble Beach at age 44.

Dawson put together an investment group to build an 18-hole course on the grounds of a dude ranch 10 miles from downtown Palm Springs, literally in the middle of the desert. Golf notables from Ben Hogan to Byron Nelson told Dawson and his group that they were crazy. How could you get grass to grow on sand in the middle of a dry desert? Who would travel 10 miles to play a wind-blown, sandy course when they could stay in Palm Springs to play O'Donnell?

They also scoffed at the notion of selling home lots on Thunderbird's course to those weighing Palm Springs as a getaway from Los Angeles. Who would buy such a home so far from town?

Dawson had the last laugh.

Through his membership at the well-heeled Lakeside Country Club in Los Angeles, Dawson invited some of the top celebrities in the world to visit Thunderbird. Dawson's cronies from Lakeside eagerly put up $2,000 each for choice lots on the course, and the early membership list at the course included Hope and Crosby, band leader and comedian Phil Harris, songwriters Hoagy Carmichael and Jimmy Van Heusen, western star Randolph Scott, television stars Lucille Ball and Desi Arnaz, entertainers Edgar Bergen, Esther Williams, Dick Powell and June Allyson, Gen. Omar Bradley and baseball star Ralph Kiner and his wife, tennis pro Nancy Chaffee.

Also on the list: Hogan, who had laughed at the project.

BELOW LEFT: Lucille Ball often visited the El Mirador Hotel in the mid-thirties. In the 1950s, she and husband Desi Arnaz built a home at Thunderbird Country Club while "I Love Lucy" brought them into the living rooms of America. *Courtesy Palm Springs Historical Society, John Miller*

BELOW: Songwriter Hoagy Carmichael was one of the Thunderbird Country Club's earliest residents. *Courtesy Rancho Mirage Public Library*

"It was like a bunch of kids having fun," Dolores Hope recalled. "And everyone loved golf. Everyone who was there was crazy about golf. Everyone felt the same way."

When Thunderbird opened in January 1951, it was an immediate hit. It earned rave reviews for its design and a lifestyle that incorporated golf with the wide-open spaces of an unspoiled desert. The celebrities brought fame to Thunderbird. But just as important to the desert and future of golf locally was the CEO profile drawn to Thunderbird.

"It might have been the wealthiest membership in the country," said Eddie Susalla, an assistant to head pro Jimmy Hines when Thunderbird opened. "We had the president of American Airlines, the head of Swanson Foods, people with Hyatt hotels and the head of Ford."

Ernest Breech, the chairman of Ford Motor Co., so loved his new club in the desert that when Ford introduced a new model for the 1955 season, Breech slapped the name of his desert course on it. The first Ford Thunderbird in the desert was presented to Dawson and his wife, Velma, who created the star puppet of the Howdy Dowdy show.

While many of the Thunderbird members were famous, Hope and Crosby had achieved crossover status as celebrities and star amateur golfers. Through their love of the game, Hope and Crosby had become identifiable with the biggest names in pro golf. That was reinforced as the two hopscotched around the country during World War II, playing golf exhibitions at war bond rallies.

"They would play with Byron Nelson, Jimmy Demaret, whoever, and they used to draw huge crowds," said Dwayne Netland, a writer for Golf Digest who would later collaborate with Hope on the book, "Bob Hope's Confessions of a Hooker: My Lifelong Love Affair with Golf."

"Pro golf was hurting badly, and whenever a guy like Hope or Crosby or anyone of that stature would play, it was a tremendous help."

Perhaps the strangest of Hope's golf collaborations and friendships was with Hogan, the venerable legend of golf's early years in the U.S. Hope was a clown and always looking for an opening for a joke or jab.

In contrast, Hogan was ice-cold serious, saying little on the course and rarely knowing what his playing partner that day was doing.

If Hope was golf's court jester, Hogan was the game's intimidator. Yet, the two became great friends, with Hope crediting Hogan for significant improvements in the comedian's game.

BELOW: Jack Benny, Ben Hogan and Benny's wife, Mary Livingstone, in the 1950s. Hogan took the head professional job at the Tamarisk Country Club that opened in 1952, just one year after Thunderbird. Jack Benny was a member at the Tamarisk. *Courtesy Palm Springs Historical Society*

The friendship of Hope and Hogan blossomed when Hogan agreed to take the head professional job at Tamarisk Country Club. It opened in 1952, just one year after Thunderbird, where Hope was a member.

Tamarisk developed into a club for the Jewish members at Thunderbird, including the Marx Brothers, Danny Kaye and Jack Benny. Hogan took the head pro job, mostly a ceremonial position, when it was common for even big-name pros to have jobs at country clubs in the winter, then play the tour in the summer.

The warm weather in the winter allowed Hogan to keep playing in those months and continue working on the rehabilitation of his legs, which had been badly crushed when his car hit a bus head-on in early 1949 on a foggy Texas road.

Hope and Hogan played often together, with the comedian being tutored by the star player.

But even the seriousness of Hogan didn't completely rub off on the clown prince of golf. Asked once what he was doing to improve his game, Hope replied, "I was down standing in the road today waiting for a Greyhound to hit me."

"They were good friends. Ben was a very, very sweet man," Dolores Hope said. "He had a nice sense of humor. He just looked like he had a machine gun in his golf bag when he was on the course."

Seeing Hope and Hogan in the same foursome might have been special in many places, but it was just another pairing in the growing desert golf scene. The celebrities could play golf with the regular club membership – if CEOs and presidents of major corporations could be called regular membership – and transcend the Hollywood label. In the desert, everyone was just a golfer.

It was this atmosphere of celebrities, top-name pros and well-heeled amateurs that the organizers of the first Palm Springs Golf Classic in 1960 were counting on. The meeting on the Thunderbird driving range in 1959 and more discussions in the following months produced a

massive and unique tournament.

Four courses – Thunderbird, Tamarisk, Indian Wells and Bermuda Dunes country clubs – would participate in the tour's only five-day, 90-hole, four-course event. Each club would be played once during the event by a pro and his three-player amateur team. After 72 holes, the pro field would be cut and a pros-only final round would be played at Thunderbird.

Additionally, each club would put up $12,500 for a $50,000 purse, more than three times the purse of the old Thunderbird Invitational.

If the Palm Springs tournament was different from every other event on tour, it also meant there was no blueprint for how to conduct such a far-flung enterprise.

ABOVE: Harpo Marx, one of the first members at the new Tamarisk Country Club when it opened in 1952, is campaigning at the club for John F. Kennedy, circa 1960. *Courtesy Rancho Mirage Public Library*

The unenviable task of devising the format fell to Bob Rosburg. He was the 1959 PGA champion who was a part-time desert resident and also president of the tour's tournament committee in 1959.

"Ernie Dunlevie, John Curci and a few people came up to me and said, 'We'd like to have something different. Can you figure something out?' I said I don't know, what do you have in mind?" Rosburg said in an interview before his 2009 death.

Rosburg was hailed as a child golf prodigy in the San Francisco area. His most famous moment before the 1959 PGA victory probably came when, as a 12-year-old, he beat baseball legend Ty Cobb in a match of the 1939 club championship at The Olympic Club. Cobb, never

ABOVE: Ben Shearer and Milt Hicks, two of the founding board members of the 1960 tournament and two giants in desert golf history. *Courtesy Bob Hope Classic archives*

RIGHT: Bob Rosburg, the 1959 PGA champion and later the 1972 Hope winner, is credited with helping devise the format that allowed the Hope to use four courses over five days with 512 players. It is a format that has been used every year of the tournament. *Courtesy Bob Hope Classic archives*

OPPOSITE TOP: Early tournament committee, circa 1962. From left, seated, Ed Vines, Bermuda Dunes; Charles Prince, tournament chairman; Charles Kasmer, tournament coordinator. Standing, Warren Orlick, Eldorado; Walter Burkemo, Eldorado; Eddie Susalla, Indian Wells; Claude Harmon, Thunderbird; Elly Vines, Tamarisk. *Courtesy Bob Hope Classic archives*

OPPOSITE BOTTOM: Classic board members Ernie Dunlevie, Eddie Susalla and Milt Hicks share an early golf cart with Susalla's son, Scott. *Courtesy Bob Hope Classic archives*

the most stable of competitors in baseball or anything else, was said to be so humiliated and infuriated by the loss that he stormed off the course never to return.

Rosburg also was known as one of the more intelligent pros on tour, a whiz with numbers and organization. The committee for the new tournament dispatched Rosburg to a cottage at Bermuda Dunes Country Club. Armed with only a notepad and colored pencils, he ducked inside, guided only by general information from the tournament about how the event was to be run.

"Three days later, I had it all figured out. And it has never changed," Rosburg said.

Rosburg's solution was for pros to have two early tee times and two late tee times in the first four days of pro-am competition, with two rounds starting on the first tee and two on the 10th tee. The rotation had to take into consideration the needs of television for the weekend, as well as the pace of play on each of the four courses.

That meant 32 pros and 32 amateur teams on each course, for a total of 128 pros and 384 amateurs or 512 total golfers.

To run the tournament, each of the four clubs involved in 1960 put three members on the Classic board. All loved golf and hoped the tournament would succeed. Perhaps the most important member was a true desert original, Milt Hicks.

Hicks was the closest thing there was to a native of the desert, though he was actually born in San Francisco in 1914. By 1915, Hicks, his mother, father and older brother moved to a homestead in Desert Hot Springs, just north of Palm Springs.

The Hicks family was one of the most important in the desert in the early years, with Milt's father, Alva, helping in the fight to incorporate Palm Springs in 1938. Milt Hicks had a good childhood, attending prep school in San Diego and college in Los Angeles. But he returned to the desert and forged a reputation as one of the area's biggest supporters of the burgeoning golf scene.

An early member at Thunderbird, Hicks later was one of the original backers of Indian Wells Country Club. He also exhibited extraordinary organizational and promotional skills, making him a natural to run tournaments. He was the chairman of the 1955 and 1959 Ryder Cup matches and could be counted on as at least a volunteer for any tournament that came around.

Hicks became known as "Mr. Golf," an impressive title for an area that was wrapping itself in the sport.

Another key member representing Indian Wells was Desi Arnaz, husband in life and on television to Lucille Ball. Arnaz and Ball were early members at Thunderbird. Arnaz later joined in the original investment group at Indian Wells.

While Arnaz played the talented but occasionally confused band leader Ricky Ricardo in "I Love Lucy,"

Starting Times and Pairings

February 5-6
1960

•

BERMUDA DUNES

INDIAN WELLS

TAMARISK

THUNDERBIRD

ABOVE: A souvenir button from the "$100,000" Desert Classic in 1960. *Courtesy Bob Hope Classic archives*

LEFT: Memorabilia from the 1960 Classic
Courtesy Bob Hope Classic archives

TOP: Desi Arnaz, an original tournament board member and founding member of Indian Wells Country Club with Debbie Reynolds, the 1962 Classic Queen.
Courtesy Bob Hope Classic archives

he was actually a shrewd executive who turned Desilu Productions into one of the largest and most profitable in Hollywood. It was safe to say, however, that Arnaz was a better businessman than he was a golfer.

"Desi couldn't play at all," said Susalla, who moved from Thunderbird to Indian Wells and is credited with the design of the first 18 holes at the new club. "I could have taught him forever, and he never was going to get much better."

Clearly, a man with Arnaz's entertainment connections could come in handy for a new tournament looking for a television deal.

"God bless him, he tried hard," Dunlevie recalled. "We were in a meeting at Tamarisk, and Desi called and said, 'I think I've got it locked in at $50,000.' That's when we decided to raise the purse. Our only obligation under the contract with the PGA was for a purse of $52,000. So, we said let's raise it to $100,000."

The March 1959 headlines in The Desert Sun trumpeted that the world's first $100,000 tournament would be played in the desert in 1960. The story also said Arnaz was "trying to get television coverage for the four-day event, which could add another $50,000 to the purse."

The trouble was Arnaz's ironclad deal for $50,000 that he had reported to the board wasn't actually locked in at all, and the entire package eventually collapsed.

Board members, saddled by their hasty decision to announce the purse, scrambled for a quick deal. But the best they could muster was a $5,000 pact with Los Angeles television station KTTV, which provided coverage from the 18th hole of all four courses on Saturday and coverage of the 17th and 18th holes at Thunderbird on Sunday. It is believed to be the first time television provided coverage from four courses on the same day.

Tour players told the tournament not to worry about staying with the original $100,000 pledge. Even though media reports during the tournament still talked about a $100,000 purse, the tournament had actually reduced it to $70,000.

Nevertheless, the financial troubles had begun.

The first Palm Springs Golf Classic began play on Feb. 3, 1960. If the purse and television contracts had been rough spots in the road, the tournament itself seemed to run smoothly enough.

The new event even managed a bit of déjà vu. Palmer, who had won the final Thunderbird Invitational in 1959

with a final-round 62, shot rounds of 67-73-67-66-65 for a sizzling 22-under 338 total and a three-shot victory over Fred Hawkins.

Hope played in the tournament that would eventually bear his name, as did board member Arnaz and other desert celebrities.

While Palmer earned $12,000 for the victory, the tournament's real prize was an offer of $50,000 to any pro making a hole-in-one. The offer was a huge one at the time, so big that the tournament had Lloyd's of London insure it against the possibility of a competition ace.

The tournament needed all that insurance and then some. Joe Campbell, a 24-year-old pro and 1955 NCAA individual golf champion for Purdue University, grabbed the bonus money the first year. In the third round, Campbell hammered a 3-iron toward the green of the 205-yard fifth hole at Tamarisk for the big-money ace.

While the tournament went smoothly thanks to Rosburg's rotation, the financial problems were mounting. Even the $5,000 for television coverage turned out to be a loss. It cost the tournament $8,000 just to set up the TV equipment.

"We had bragged that the first year all the money was going to go to charity. But we wound up losing $65,000," Dunlevie said.

The tournament faced a crushing debt from which it probably wouldn't recover. Again, the powerful nature of the people who populated the desert at the time gave the tournament a break: A member at Tamarisk Country Club also served on the board of a bank in Beverly Hills.

"He said, 'If you guys will sign personal guarantees, we'll loan you the money to pay it off.' So we paid off the $65,000," Dunlevie said.

The board had covered the purse and costs for running and televising the tournament. But that

LEFT: Arnold Palmer shows his winning score from the inaugural tournament in 1960. The score would stand as a tournament record for 17 years. *Courtesy Bob Hope Classic archives*

BELOW: Joe Campbell shows off part of the $50,000 he won for making a hole-in-one in the 1960 tournament. Classic Queen Gail Davis and Classic board member Milt Hicks celebrate with Campbell. *Courtesy Bob Hope Classic archives*

left nothing for the charitable donations the tournament had ballyhooed in the months before the event. There was talk of shutting down the tournament after just one year, fueled by the absence of fans at the debut.

"I think we had more directors on the golf courses than we had gallery," Dunlevie said.

Particularly angry at the financial debacle were the members of the clubs who had backed the tournament. Faced with the end of their tournament after one year, the board of directors held a critical meeting. In either a bold or a foolish move, the board chose bravado over retreat.

"We decided to have a big luncheon at the El Mirador Hotel and give away money to charity," Dunlevie said. "So we borrowed another $15,000."

The luncheon was a success, and the desert charities were impressed with the $15,000 they thought were the profits from the tournament. The enthusiastic response to the donations was enough to convince the board not to kill off the tournament.

The Palm Springs Golf Classic had survived its first year, if just barely. Better days and bigger challenges were to come in the next few years. ∎

LEFT: Golfers putting behind the El Mirador Hotel, Palm Springs, 1950s. The hotel was the site of a big luncheon following the 1960 Classic during which the Classic gave a $15,000 check to charity. *Courtesy Palm Springs Historical Society*

OPPOSITE: Classic board member Milt Hicks seems more interested in Beverly Hillbillies Donna Douglas than he is in former President Dwight Eisenhower or fellow board member Robert McCulloch in the first round of the 1964 Classic. *Courtesy Bob Hope Classic archives*

ABOVE: Billy Maxwell, 1961 Classic Champion.
Courtesy Bob Hope Classic archives

RIGHT: Barbara and Jack Nicklaus and Eddie Susalla pose with the Eisenhower Trophy after Nicklaus' 18-hole play-off victory at Indian Wells over Gary Player in the 1963 Classic. Because of the 18-hole playoff, Nicklaus and Player each played 108 holes, the longest tournament in Classic history. *Courtesy Bob Hope Classic archives*

Hope for the Desert

··

As the 1960s began, the fledgling Palm Springs Golf Classic tournament looked enviously to the Monterey Peninsula and the smashing success of Bing Crosby's pro-am golf events.

The Palm Springs tournament debuted in 1960 and had its share of celebrity players, most of whom were members at the five country club courses played in the event: Thunderbird, Indian Wells, Bermuda Dunes,

Tamarisk and the newly added Eldorado.

But Crosby was wowing America with his star power.

Crosby had hosted a professional-amateur tournament since 1937, starting at Rancho Santa Fe Country Club in San Diego. Sam Snead won the first two of what would become known as the Crosby Clambake.

Like many sporting events, Crosby's tournament was interrupted by World War II and wasn't played from 1943-46. It re-appeared in 1947 as a 54-hole event on glorious courses – Pebble Beach, Cypress Point and Monterey Peninsula Country Club – in Northern California.

ABOVE: Bing Crosby never played in the Classic, but did serve as the inspiration for board members Ernie Dunlevie and Milt Hicks to pursue Bob Hope as host of the Desert Classic. *Courtesy Bob Hope Classic archives*

LEFT: In this promotional photo for the 1966 Hope tournament, Gary Player, Arnold Palmer and Jack Nicklaus promote the event. The three were in the Coachella Valley to film a segment of their popular Big Three Golf television series at Indian Wells Country Club. *Courtesy Bob Hope Classic archives*

The game's best played in the Clambake, from Snead to Ben Hogan to Byron Nelson, all of whom won the event after the move from San Diego. Crosby's name and friendship with celebrities from all areas of show business attracted the stars to the tournament, which featured a format of one pro paired with one amateur.

Palm Springs' officials knew something was missing in their tournament. They sought a spark that would make the tournament more than another winter stop for the touring pros looking to win a few dollars and catch a tan after a winter in the Northeast.

That something, the board of directors believed, was the star quality that enveloped Crosby's tournament.

That star, they determined, was Bob Hope.

Hope was among the celebrities who played in the early years of the Palm Springs event as well as Crosby's tournament. But his participation in the Palm Springs event was no greater than other celebrities such as songwriter Hoagy Carmichael, the Marx Brothers or baseball great Ralph Kiner.

In 1962, Ernie Dunlevie, a board member, and Milt Hicks, tournament president, trekked up the California coast to visit Crosby's tournament. After seeing the Crosby effect firsthand, they hatched a plan: Convince Hope to lend his name to the Palm Springs tournament.

With Hope as the Palm Springs tournament's host, Hicks and Dunlevie were convinced they could attract more sponsors and bigger celebrities, stars who specifically traveled to play in the tournament instead of just walking out their back door to play the event.

The idea of hitching the tournament onto Hope's star was indeed a natural. But Dunlevie and Hicks knew getting Hope to agree would be difficult. Hope had an obvious love for the game and the desert, but he also was one of Hollywood's busiest.

From 1960-64, Hope starred in six movies, including "The Road to Hong Kong," the seventh and final "Road" picture teaming Hope and Crosby, and two movies with Lucille Ball.

If he wasn't filming a movie, Hope was doing a television variety special. One, 1961's "The World of Bob Hope," included footage of Hope playing in the Palm Springs tournament that year.

If it wasn't a television special, Hope was touring America, doing fairs and fundraisers.

And if he wasn't barnstorming this country, he was entertaining American military troops somewhere around the world.

It was a wonder Hope ever squeezed in a round of golf at his beloved Lakeside Country Club in Los Angeles or at Thunderbird or Tamarisk in Palm Springs. What chance did Hicks and Dunlevie have of convincing this human whirlwind to host a week-long golf tournament?

Their wooing began one day in 1963 when Hicks heard that Hope was playing a round at O'Donnell Golf Club in downtown Palm Springs. That kind of news spread easily and quickly in the small village that Palm Springs still was.

O'Donnell was the oldest existing club in the desert and the hotspot for celebrity golfers before Thunderbird and Tamarisk opened in the early 1950s, and Hope was still a regular player at the nine-hole course.

Hicks called Dunlevie to set up a double-team assault on Hope.

"Milt said, 'Why don't you come down and we'll grab him in the locker room,' " Dunlevie said. "So I did. We broached the subject to him, and he said 'Gee, I hadn't really given it any thought. I'll have to think about it.' "

While Hope brushed off the first pitch, Hicks and Dunlevie knew they had aroused a little interest and perhaps even a little jealousy in Hope.

"It didn't appear to be too difficult of a project because there was always a lot of competition between Hope and Crosby," Dunlevie said. "And we felt after talking to him, we had our foot in the door."

A rivalry was natural between two huge stars, even close friends such as Hope and Crosby. It extended to the golf course where Crosby was considered the better golfer, despite Hope's dedication to the game.

"Bob used to say golf was his real business," Dolores Hope said. "And he was good, very good. He was down to a 4 handicap. Bing would always beat him, though."

Dunlevie and Hicks were fortunate to have an ally in their quest for Hope – the comedian's wife, Dolores.

"Bob came home one day and said, 'You know, they want to change the tournament and they want to call it the Bob Hope,' " Dolores recalled. "He said, 'I don't want to do that.' I said I thought it would be great because Bing's got his tournament up there, and I think that would be a lot of fun.

"He said, 'You think so?' I said, 'Yes, I think that would be a lot of fun because we both love golf.'"

Two versions of how Hope agreed to host the Palm Springs tournament exist.

One is that Hicks and Dunlevie, joined by tournament board members, continued to pressure Hope to join the tournament throughout 1963. It all culminated one day when, purely by accident, Hope, Hicks and Dunlevie found themselves on the same Western Airlines commuter flight from Palm Springs to Los Angeles. It was a popular business route for the growing number of L.A. residents who were discovering the desert as a second home.

Hicks went to work right away. He talked his way into the first-class section where Hope was sitting and then described the benefits for Hope and the tournament if the comedian were to lend his name to the event.

Maybe it was Hicks' impassioned plea or the idea of having a tournament like Crosby. By the end of the 30-minute flight to Los Angeles, Hope was convinced. He agreed to play an active role in the tournament, including having his name on the event.

Hope's version of what happened was always a little different.

He admitted that Hicks and Dunlevie approached him first and that he was intrigued with the prospect of

matching Crosby with a PGA event. But Hope felt he was too busy and turned down the offer.

Where Hope's version differs is in what happened next. Hope said Hicks and Dunlevie returned, seeking his help in getting a title sponsor or at least someone to help underwrite the cost of the tournament.

Hope arguably was not only the country's most popular entertainer at the time but also a well-paid commercial spokesman for a variety of products and services. His most high-profile endorsement deal was with Chrysler.

ABOVE: James Garner, Billy Casper and Bob Hope being interviewed by Lindsay Nelson in 1965.
Courtesy Bob Hope Classic archives

ABOVE: From left, Otto Graham, quarterback for the Cleveland Browns; Betty Grable and Arnold Palmer in the 1960s. Graham was among the big names Bob Hope was able to bring to the Classic.
Courtesy Historical Society of Palm Desert

OPPOSITE TOP: Danny Thomas, Bob Hope and Casey Stengel at the 1966 tournament.
Courtesy Historical Society of Palm Desert

OPPOSITE BOTTOM: Dick Martin, Phyllis Diller and Bob Hope look on as Doug Sanders prepares to tee off, circa 1967. *Courtesy Bob Hope Classic archives*

"We were not involved with golf, but we were involved with Bob Hope," said Ed Heorodt, an advertising and promotions executive for Chrysler for 22 years. "We sponsored Chrysler Theater back in the middle 1960s, and they had the Bob Hope musical variety shows. So, we knew Bob Hope.

"I was sitting in my boss' office one day and he had a call from Bob Hope (who) said, 'I just had a call from some people in the desert who want to put my name on a golf tournament. What's involved?' My boss said, 'I'll do it. I'll sponsor it on TV as long as we are the sole advertiser.'

"So in 1964, NBC had the rights, and we signed up for the tournament. And that's how Chrysler became involved."

Whichever version of the story you believe, everything seemed set for Hope to debut as the tournament host for the 1964 tournament. That was until an emergency meeting of the tournament board just months before the event.

Tournament president Bob McCulloch "called me one day to talk about continuing the tournament," Dunlevie said. "And he said, 'When I finish telling you what I have to tell you, there may not be another tournament.' "

Through a series of miscalculations on the part of tournament officials, and because of some of the early struggles the event had meeting purses and doling out funds to charities, the Palm Springs Golf Classic was informed by the Internal Revenue Service that it owed $110,000 in back taxes.

The visit from the IRS was a dire threat to the future of the event.

Fortunately for the tournament and Hope, the IRS problem surfaced before any official announcement of his participation in the tournament. Wary of any unwanted publicity, the decision was quickly made to keep Hope's name off the tournament until the tax problem was resolved.

The tournament's future hung on how the tax problem could be paid off. Fortunately for the tournament, most of the country clubs involved with the event were populated by rich and powerful people – or, at least people who had connections with rich and powerful people.

Those relationships paid off when a member at Eldorado Country Club put the tournament board in touch with Dana Latham, who was no ordinary tax attorney. Latham had been the commissioner of the IRS during the Eisenhower administration and had returned to private practice in Los Angeles with the law firm of Latham and Watkins.

"He offered his services. He said, 'I go back to Washington two or three times a year, I'll look into it,'" Dunlevie said.

"We went to the meeting, and Latham said, 'According to the section of the Code so-and-so, which I wrote …,' I felt lots better right then," said board member Paul Jenkins. "Then he picked up the phone while we were there and called Irving Shapiro, who was head of the IRS under Lyndon Johnson. I felt even better then."

As word of the IRS problem filtered into the desert community, the Hope board issued a press release downplaying what was actually a serious matter.

"Contrary to an earlier report, the Classic board did not receive the IRS preliminary report as a "complete surprise.

"The board has been aware of the situation since 1960 and conversant with a similar ruling affecting the Bing Crosby tournament made several years ago," the June 26, 1964, news release stated. "Obviously, this did not adversely affect the Crosby Clambake or result in the cancellation of that event."

The answer Latham came up with was complicated and stayed in place for more than 30 years. Instead of one nonprofit organization, the tournament was organized into two nonprofits. The arm of the event known as Desert Charities would raise the money from the tournament. The money was then turned over to The Palm Desert Foundation, which in turn handed out the cash to the charities. It was a legal detour that saved professional golf in Palm Springs.

For his efforts, Latham was named an honorary board member of the tournament.

While details of the new system were worked out, Hope was becoming a bit anxious about lending his name to the tournament. After all, it had been months since he agreed to host the tournament and bring Chrysler on board.

Hope told his longtime agent, Jimmy Saphier, to make a call and check on the status. Was the tournament still serious about having Hope involved? Was there even going to be a tournament?

Dunlevie explained to Saphier that the tournament was close to resolving the IRS mess and assured the agent it still wanted Hope. Saphier agreed it was best that Hope's name not be involved in anything close to a tax scandal. Call when you get things straightened out for good, Saphier told tournament leaders.

One month later, Dunlevie traveled to Los Angeles to meet with Saphier. Details of the agreement to change the tournament name to the Bob Hope Desert Classic were hammered out at Saphier's Sunset Boulevard office. After lunch, the two returned to Saphier's office, and Dunlevie learned just what kind of impact Hope could have on the tournament.

"Jimmy said, 'What kind of money do you get from NBC?' I said we are getting a $50,000 rights fee," Dunlevie said. "He said, 'That's pretty good. What else should I know?' I said I think you should know that we should be getting $100,000. He said why. I said that's what they are paying Crosby.

"He said, 'Well, if they are paying Crosby $100,000, we should get $100,000.' "

Saphier picked up the phone and called Crosby's brother, Everett, who was the crooner's agent and was

involved with the Clambake. Everett Crosby confirmed that his brother's tournament did indeed receive twice what the Palm Springs tournament was getting.

"Jimmy then called NBC, and of course we got our $100,000," Dunlevie said. "So, we got a $50,000 bump the very day that we got Bob's name."

More changes were almost as immediate. Hope took an active role in shoring up what had become a sagging list of celebrities in the event. His phone calls yielded such big names as Kirk Douglas, Lawrence Welk, Bob Newhart, Cleveland Browns quarterback Otto Graham, Notre Dame football coach Ara Parseghian and baseball manager and philosopher Casey Stengel playing in the tournament.

Hope also put his talents toward producing the tournament's black-tie ball, which now had the best featured act and master of ceremonies in the country – Hope himself.

"By that time, we were probably suffering a little bit in getting celebrities," Dunlevie said. "After Bob was involved, if we wanted someone to play and we hadn't heard from them, Bob would pick up the phone and the next thing you know you had a commitment."

One change was a little more cosmetic. In an effort to identify Hope with the tournament as much as possible, the tournament commissioned the design of a new logo. Artists took advantage of Hope's most notable physical feature, his prominent ski nose. The design featured a golf ball teed up on the tip of an exaggerated nose of a profile of a grinning Hope.

Another idea directly from Hope was the addition

ABOVE: Hope joins Alice Faye for a dance during the 1980 Classic Ball. *Courtesy Bob Hope Classic archives*

RIGHT: Bob and Dolores Hope take time for a dance during the 1980 Classic ball. *Courtesy Bob Hope Classic archives*

FAR RIGHT: Old "hoofers" Bob Hope and Sammy Davis Jr., entertain at a Classic Ball in 1981. Davis was the host of a PGA tournament event in Hartford, Conn. *Courtesy Bob Hope Classic archives*

OPPOSITE BOTTOM LEFT: Arnold Palmer, amateur Jim Crooker, Hope Board members Steve Morton and Ernie Dunlevie share a moment at the Hope Classic Ball in the 1990s. *Courtesy Bob Hope Classic archives*

OPPOSITE RIGHT: Dinah Shore and Vic Damone perform during a Classic Ball in the 1980s. They were accompanied by Les Brown and the Band of Renown. Shore hosted her own desert tournament on the LPGA Tour, until she died in 1994. *Courtesy Bob Hope Classic archives*

ABOVE: Hope, always up for a quick "soft shoe," performs at a Classic Ball with his longtime friend and San Diego Chargers owner, Alex Spanos, in the early 1980s.

of a little sex appeal to the tournament. It already had four young, shapely women who would walk around the tournament in tight tops that proclaimed "Palm," "Springs," "Golf" and "Classic."

"Of course when Hope came along, they became the Bob Hope Classic girls," Dunlevie said. "The first year,

Hope said, 'Why don't we have a Classic queen?' Well, how do we get a Classic queen? He said, 'Don't worry about it.' That's how that started."

For the 1965 tournament, the queen was an attractive young redheaded starlet named Jill St. John, just gaining her reputation in Hollywood. She would be followed in

ABOVE: A contestant badge from the 1969 Bob Hope Desert Classic showing the logo designed to identify Hope with the tournament. *Courtesy Bob Hope Classic archives*

RIGHT: Bob Hope celebrated his first year as host of the tournament in 1965. Here, Hope and 1965 Classic Queen Jill St. John are interviewed by NBC's Lindsay Nelson. *Courtesy Bob Hope Classic archives*

OPPOSITE LEFT: The Hope Girls, from left, are Wanda Acuna, Lori Ruehle, and Monica Getchell in 1985. *Courtesy Desert Sun archives*

OPPOSITE TOP RIGHT: Chuck Connors and Arnold Palmer with the Hope Girls Scarlett Huenergardt, Janet Rogers and Chris Holliday in 1968. *Courtesy Bob Hope Classic archives*

OPPOSITE MIDDLE RIGHT: A birthday cake presented by Lori Ruehle, Laurl McLaughlin and Kimberly Charles-worth, to Bob Hope in celebration of the 25th Bob Hope Classic in 1984. *Courtesy Desert Sun archives*

OPPOSITE BOTTOM RIGHT: 1994 Classic champion Peter Jacobsen with Hope Girls Michelle Watters, Sandra Howard and Heather Applin. *Courtesy Bob Hope Classic archives*

the role by such curvaceous stars as "I Dream of Jeanie's" Barbara Eden and Linda Carter, who starred as Wonder Woman on TV. At the time, Carter was the reigning Miss World, and several others who held that title served as Classic queens through the years.

"We never would have gotten those people without Hope," Dunlevie said.

Other changes helped inject more pizzazz into the tournament. Tournament directors now found themselves driving courtesy cars from Chrysler and sporting custom blazers from Hart Schaffner Marx, another long-time commercial partner of Hope.

ABOVE: Bob Hope seems to enjoy the attention from 1971 Classic Queen Gloria Loring and Irene Ryan, "Granny" from the Beverly Hillbillies. *Courtesy Bob Hope Classic archives*

LEFT: Efrem Zimbalist, Jr., Miss World Lynda Carter, who was cast as Wonder Woman, and Arnold Palmer, 1973. *Courtesy Bob Hope Classic archives*

OPPOSITE: One of the most famous additions to the tournament was a ski-nosed golf cart in the image of Bob Hope. 1970 Classic Queen Barbara Eden jokes with Hope about the resemblance. *Courtesy Bob Hope Classic archives*

"There were a lot of perks that came with Bob," Dunlevie said.

Even without Hope on board, the Palm Springs tournament had grown from its first debt-plagued year. The loans and bluffing after the first tournament saved what in a single year had become the tour's most original format.

Sandwiched into a West Coast winter swing that included events such as the Crosby, the Lucky Open in San Francisco and stops in Los Angeles, San Diego, Hawaii and Phoenix, the Palm Springs tournament offered features no other tournament had.

While the Crosby had three courses, the Hope had

LEFT: A picture of style, Hope dances off the green in the 1970s. *Courtesy Bob Hope Classic archives*

BELOW: Eisenhower Trophy presentation in 1966. *Courtesy Bob Hope Classic archives*

OPPOSITE LEFT: A star-studded group celebrates Arnold Palmer's third win in the Hope in 1968 at Bermuda Dunes Country Club. The presentations include former president Dwight Eisenhower (left), playoff runner-up Deane Beman, California Gov. Ronald Reagan, Hope and Palmer. *Courtesy Bob Hope Classic archives*

OPPOSITE TOP RIGHT: Bob Hope with the Eisenhower trophy, 1970. In the background at right is California Gov. Ronald Reagan. *Courtesy Bob Hope Classic archives*

OPPOSITE BOTTOM RIGHT: Bob Hope sitting on the floor of the press tent in 1972. *Courtesy Bob Hope Classic archives*

four. Each tournament had some form of a pro-am, with the Crosby's format linking one pro with one amateur for the duration of the event. In the Hope, each pro was hooked up with a three-player amateur team for the first four days of the tournament. Even the event's five-day, 90-hole format was unlike any other tournament. The idea was to break away from the mold of the 54- or 72-hole stroke-play tournaments that to this day often make one PGA Tour stop look exactly like the one the week before or the week after.

Hope's first tournament as host in 1965 proved to be a memorable one. Billy Casper made a two-foot birdie putt on the 18th hole at Bermuda Dunes to edge Tommy Aaron and a charging Palmer, already a legend at the tournament.

Hope was on hand to congratulate Casper, as was one of Hope's closest friends, former President Dwight Eisenhower. The retired general who spearheaded the Normandy Invasion on D-Day had a winter home at Eldorado Country Club. He was the first to greet Casper after the victory, saying, "That was a real knee-knocker you just made."

What other tournament could boast of a former president shaking hands with the winner?

Immediately, Hope's involvement was paying dividends, Dunlevie said.

"There is no question that the tournament, from the minute Bob Hope became associated with it, it doubled in importance." ■

ABOVE: During the 1960s and 1970s the Bob Hope Classic drew large crowds, as seen on the 18th hole at Indian Wells. *Courtesy Bob Hope Classic archives*

RIGHT: Gallery at Indian Wells watching the Bob Hope Classic, circa 1970. *Courtesy Bob Hope Classic archives*

OPPOSITE TOP LEFT: View from the Santa Rosa Mountains to the 18th green at Indian Wells County Club in 1984. *Courtesy Bob Hope Classic archives*

OPPOSITE BOTTOM LEFT: Scenic shot of the fairways and flora of La Quinta Country Club.
Courtesy Bob Hope Classic archives

OPPOSITE RIGHT: Gallery surrounds the 18th green at La Quinta County Club during the 1983 tounament.
Courtesy Bob Hope Classic archives

Eisenhower: The general, golfer and medical center

*T*he perpetual trophy for the Bob Hope Chrysler Classic is a rather nondescript putter mounted on a sterling silver panel attached to a large slab of wood.

Hanging in the Hope tournament office on the grounds of world-renowned Eisenhower Medical Center in Rancho Mirage, it features the names of each winner and year they won.

What makes the trophy special is the signature engraved on the putter: Dwight David Eisenhower, the former supreme commander of allied forces in World War II and the 34th president of the United States.

Eisenhower never played in Bob Hope's PGA Tour event, which debuted in the final full year of Eisenhower's second term as president in 1960. But he became a constant figure in the tournament's early years, cheering on winners, developing friendships with players and doing as much – if not more – than Hope and rising star Arnold Palmer to popularize the game in the 1950s and early 1960s.

"I never knew what his handicap was, but he had played a lot of golf while he was in the military," said former President Gerald Ford, who followed Eisenhower's path into the White House and onto the golf course.

"He had a little putting green at the White House, and it included a little sand trap next to it."

Here was a president who kept his short game sharp while shepherding the country through the Cold War. This was the president who made annual pilgrimages to Augusta National, and, as a member of the club, argued that a tree on the fabled course's 17th hole should be cut down only to have the offending tree become forever known as the Eisenhower Tree.

The connection between Bob Hope and Eisenhower, not surprisingly, began during World War II, and golf

was at the center of the meeting.

In his book, "Bob Hope's Confessions of a Hooker: My Lifelong Love Affair with Golf," Hope recalls being with his team of entertainers in North Africa on one of the first of his many trips to perform for the allied forces. Eisenhower was also in the area and summoned Hope for a meeting. Hope claimed the meeting began with Eisenhower asking, "So, how's your golf game?"

The two became good friends in the following years for their shared passions: devotion to U.S. troops, political beliefs and golf. Eisenhower, a centrist who could have run for president as either a Republican or a Democrat and won, rode his popularity to the White House as head of the Republican ticket in the 1952 election.

While he wasn't the first president to play golf, Eisenhower was the first to display his affection for the game so publicly. By the time he took office in 1953, Eisenhower had already been a member at Augusta National, home of the Masters, for four years.

Eisenhower and his wife, Mamie, first came to the Palm Springs area in February 1954, just over a year after he was inaugurated. Eisenhower was at home in the desert, already a GOP bastion and a growing stronghold for golf.

In the following years, the Eisenhowers made several trips to the area, and Ike was naturally invited to play at every course in the desert as they opened. He played numerous rounds at Thunderbird and Tamarisk, then later at Indian Wells, Bermuda Dunes and Eldorado. When Eisenhower left office in 1961, one of his retirement homes was on the 11th fairway at Eldorado, a course that joined the Palm Springs Golf Classic rotation for the first time that year.

He was a simple man from Kansas who loved rounds of golf with a good friend and a cold beer.

"I used to actually go and sit with him in his backyard at Eldorado," Arnold Palmer said. "He always had a keg of fresh beer. He wasn't drinking much because of his

ABOVE: Dwight Eisenhower in 1963.
Courtesy Bob Hope Classic archives

OPPOSITE: President Dwight Eisenhower, board member Ernie Dunlevie and Bob Hope pose with the Eisenhower Trophy prior to the 1961 tournament.
Courtesy Bob Hope Classic archives

health. But he would sometimes have a half a glass, and I would sometimes have four or five glasses. And we would just talk about the tournament and golfers and experiences and people, just a lot of things. It was fun talk."

Palmer wasn't Eisenhower's only connection to the desert or Hope's tournament.

"Playing golf with him was just like playing golf with anybody else," said Ernie Dunlevie, tournament board member. "He'd swear like a trooper and was very competitive. He beat me and he wanted his money. He said, 'OK, you owe me $15 or $20,' or whatever it was. Yes sir, Mr. President, sir."

Eisenhower became a fixture in the early years of the Classic when his schedule allowed. Sitting behind the 18th green of the host course, Eisenhower would mingle with everyone from celebrities to the young starlets who often adorned the event. He also would participate in post-tournament ceremonies, presenting the trophy to the winner as Hope beamed.

For the 1968 tournament program, it wasn't defending champion Tom Nieporte on the cover. It was Eisenhower and Hope, both chuckling as if the comedian had just cracked a joke about a Democrat. Inside the program were pictures of the former president presenting the Eisenhower Trophy to 1965 winner Billy

Casper and 1966 winner Doug Sanders. There also were more candid shots of the former president with such stars as Pat Boone and desert resident and band leader Fred Waring.

The program also featured Eisenhower's annual letter to Hope commemorating another tournament.

"Be assured of my earnest support of any venture for the general good with which you are associated," Eisenhower wrote. "In so many fields, from the education of our young people to the morale of our troops in distant lands, you have been for so long a leading contributor to the country's well-being that such support should be expected from every American."

While Eisenhower was a huge presence at the

ABOVE: Pat Boone and Dwight Eisenhower in 1967. *Courtesy Bob Hope Classic archives*

LEFT: President Dwight Eisenhower congratulates 1967 tournament winner Tom Nieporte as tournament host Bob Hope looks on. *Courtesy Bob Hope Classic archives*

OPPOSITE TOP: Classic board members pose with President Dwight Eisenhower, who holds the tournament's perpetual trophy named after him. The putter at the top of the plaque belonged to Eisenhower. Board members include, from left, Milt Hicks, Robert McCulouch, Eddie Stantin, Ernie Dunlevie and David Holub. *Courtesy Bob Hope Classic archives*

OPPOSITE BOTTOM LEFT: From left, Paul Jenkins, President Dwight Eisenhower, Bob Hope, Doug Sanders and Arnold Palmer, during the presentation of the Eisenhower Trophy in 1966. *Courtesy Desert Sun archives*

OPPOSITE BOTTOM RIGHT: Cover of the 1968 Bob Hope Desert Classic program. *Courtesy Bob Hope Classic archives*

tournament, it was another military man who helped put it on solid organizational footing.

The job of handling the nuts and bolts of the tournament for the first six years had been handled by an executive board and tournament committees, almost as casually as you'd expect a school dance to be organized.

But the tournament was growing and changing, and adding Hope's name for the 1965 event made it more of a year-round business. The tournament started looking for a full-time director, and they found their man in a brigadier general from the Air Force named Bill Yancey.

Yancey, who was nearing retirement in 1966, was familiar with the desert. As part of his command in the 1950s and 1960s, Yancey oversaw several Air Force bases in the western United States, including March Air Force Base in Riverside, about an hour from Palm Springs.

It wasn't until years later, when documents were declassified, that the tournament discovered just what Yancey had done in some of his years at March. The man running the Hope tournament had been in charge of testing the infamous U-2 spy plane and training pilots for secret missions.

"We checked out the U-2 as a plane, the very first one that was built, and made sure that it would work," said Yancey, who still lives in the house he and his wife bought in 1966 just a few blocks from Eldorado Country Club.

"We flew over our country for a year testing the equipment and testing the airplane and training our pilots. Our air defense command never knew we were there, over our own country," Yancey added.

A man who had been instrumental in helping the U.S. spy on the Soviet Union in the most frigid of days of the Cold War was now focused on making sure Hope board members had the right blazers from Hart Shaffner Marx and the right size Florsheim shoes.

It was a job that suited Yancey quite well. While in the Air Force, Yancey had organized a six-state youth golf tournament in Alabama, and he eventually received a letter from Eisenhower thanking him for his efforts.

It was his organization and love for the game that helped take the tournament to a new level of efficiency.

"I felt very strongly that we had to have an office that was year-round. You can't start in October and November and have a tournament a month or two later when it was growing at that speed," Yancey said. "I think we did a pretty good job. We doubled the amount of money we gave to charity the first year."

Eisenhower remained a beloved figure in the country throughout the 1960s, and that included his appearance at Hope's tournament. Perhaps the greatest tribute to Eisenhower from the tournament came at the end of the 1968 event, when the final round was at Bermuda Dunes.

Yancey's connections to the military came in handy when the idea surfaced to have a musical salute to the former president. Yancey was able to get a U.S. Navy band to come to the desert from San Diego, a Marine Corps band from nearby Twentynine Palms Marine Air-Ground Combat Center and an Air Force band from Yancey's old command at March Air Force base in Riverside.

Eisenhower and his wife, Mamie, were in their customary place with Hope in the grandstands behind the 18th hole for the final round, unable to see the first fairway where the three bands were lining up in formation. When the final putt dropped on the 18th green, the bands began marching up the fairway toward the grandstands and Eisenhower.

"They played the strains of the Air Force and Army and Navy and Marine hymns," Yancey recalls. "Eisenhower was there, and tears were in his eyes. It was really quite moving."

There was just one problem. The combined bands had started marching up the fairway just moments after Palmer had made a dramatic birdie on the 18th to force a playoff with young pro Deane Beman.

Yancey suddenly found himself orchestrating a concert for Eisenhower and a playoff.

A similar tribute was planned for 1969, but Eisenhower's failing health didn't allow him to travel to Palm Springs. The World War II hero's health had been in a tailspin since he suffered a major heart attack in 1965.

In 1968, just a few months after attending what turned out to be his last Hope tournament, Eisenhower suffered another major heart attack, which ended his

BELOW: President Dwight Eisenhower and his wife, Mamie, acknowledge the crowd as Bob Hope looks on during the 1968 tournament. *Courtesy Bob Hope Classic archives*

EISENHOWER MEDICAL

public appearances. On March 28, 1969, barely a month after the 1969 Hope tournament, Eisenhower died at the Walter Reed Army Hospital in Washington, D.C.

While Eisenhower died just 10 years into the history of the tournament, his legacy to the event continues as the main beneficiary of Classic charity funds. The Eisenhower Medical Center opened officially in 1971, two years after the death of the former president.

The need for a hospital in the middle of the Coachella Valley was fueled largely by the increasing popularity of golf in the desert. New country clubs were opening at a rapid pace in the unincorporated area between Indio and Palm Springs, about 20 miles apart.

"There was a hospital in Indio, and not much of a hospital at the time, and a hospital in Palm Springs, the old army hospital that was there during the war," Dunlevie said.

"With Eldorado and Indian Wells and Bermuda Dunes developing, there was a lot of concern that if someone had a heart attack, by the time they trucked them all the way up to Palm Springs, they may not last. So, originally we were just going to start a little emergency facility."

Approached by members of the committee and other friends, Eisenhower agreed to lend his name to the project.

"Of course, then we realized you can't have Eisenhower's name on a little first-aid station. So then it

LEFT: Arnold Palmer, Jack Nicklaus and President Dwight Eisenhower at ceremonial groundbreaking at Eisenhower Medical Center, 1969.
Courtesy Bob Hope Classic archives

OPPOSITE: California Gov. Ronald Reagan participates in ground-breaking ceremonies for the Eisenhower Medical Center in Rancho Mirage, 1970. Also turning dirt are Dolores Hope, Edgar Eisenhower (Dwight's brother) and Bob Hope, who chose a different kind of instrument.
Courtesy Bob Hope Classic archives

became a big project," Dunlevie said.

Getting the land for the project was easier than most people would have believed. The committee had its eye on an 80-acre parcel on Rio Del Sol Road in Rancho Mirage.

The land happened to be owned by Bob and Dolores Hope. In fact, it might have been hard to find a chunk of land that large in the desert that wasn't either owned by Hope or was next to land owned by Hope. Ever the shrewd businessman, Hope had made the decision years earlier to put much of his money into real estate.

Hope readily agreed to donate the 80 acres to the project on the road that was later named Bob Hope Drive. He also donated something else to the project: his wife.

"He came home one day and said, 'Oh, by the way, they want to build a hospital out there and they have a group and they wanted me to be on the board, and I told them I couldn't do it, but I'm sure you would,'" Dolores Hope said.

"And I said not me. I had just gotten finished with a big project that we were doing in Los Angeles, and I was looking for a little rest.

"So Pollard Simon called me with that cute little Dallas accent and said, 'Dolores, it would be just nice to have you there. No work.' Famous last words. So that's where we started," she said.

While Dolores Hope and the rest of the hospital committee battled to get it started, Eisenhower was more than just an interested bystander. Mrs. Hope said the former president was hands-on in all aspects of the project – including the architecture. He even suggested a separate admitting entrance from the main business doors.

"He used to say that he had been in and out of so many hospitals, and he hated the idea that everyone was around and sees you," Mrs. Hope said.

Eisenhower Medical Center may be the most visible evidence of the tournament's impact on the desert, but

the fact was the tournament was becoming one of the biggest charitable organizations in the Coachella Valley.

By 1968, total contributions to desert charities surpassed $1 million. That grew to $2 million by 1971. By 1983, when contributions passed $11 million, the Hope was raising more than $1 million each year.

That flow of money continues today. Typically, the tournament generates about $1.8 million for as many as 40 local charities.

Through the 1980s and into the 1990s, the Hope was hailed as the biggest charity tournament on the PGA Tour.

Organizations as varied as food banks, Boys and Girls clubs and boxing groups continue to receive funds from the $47 million the tournament has raised through

ABOVE: Bob Hope unveiling the portrait of President Eisenhower. The president's brother, Edgar, can barely be seen in the photograph. *Courtesy Bob Hope Classic archives*

ABOVE: Recently completed Eisenhower Medical Center, 1971. *Courtesy Bob Hope Classic archives*

LEFT: Construction continues on the Eisenhower Medical Center, 1970. *Courtesy Bob Hope Classic archives*

OPPOSITE BOTTOM LEFT: Construction begins on the Eisenhower Medical Center, 1969.
Courtesy Bob Hope Classic archives

OPPOSITE RIGHT: Construction continues on the Eisenhower Medical Center, 1970. *Courtesy Bob Hope Classic archives*

the 2008 event.

And it's impossible to escape the Hope tournament's impact at Eisenhower Medical Center.

A back road into the property is John Sinn Road, named for a Hope board member. The famous Betty Ford Center is on the grounds, named for the wife of one of the tournament's favorite celebrity politicians. The Lucy Curci Cancer Center is named for the wife of board member John Curci. The Arnold Palmer Prostate Cancer Center is also there, near the Hope tournament's offices, which are a one-minute walk from the hospital's front door.

There's a reason why the medical center was dubbed, "The Hospital Built by a Golf Tournament." ∎

ABOVE: Nancy and Gov. Ronald Reagan, Pat and President Richard Nixon, Dolores and Bob Hope and Judy and Vice President Spiro Agnew at the Eisenhower Medical Center Dedication in 1971. *Courtesy Bob Hope Classic archives*

OPPOSITE: Construction continues on the Eisenhower Medical Center, 1970. *Courtesy Bob Hope Classic archives*

LEFT: Bob Hope addresses the crowd at the dedication ceremonies at Eisenhower Medical Center in 1971. In the front row of the dignitaries is First Lady Pat Nixon, Dolores Hope, California Gov. Ronald Reagan and Nancy Reagan. *Courtesy Bob Hope Classic archives*

ABOVE: The 1986 ribbon-cutting ceremonies at the Barbara Sinatra Childrens Center at Eisenhower Medical Center featured Classic board member John Sinn; California Attorney Gerneral John Van de Kamp, Barbara and Frank Sinatra, and President Ford.
Courtesy Bob Hope Classic archives

LEFT TOP: Gerald Ford helps Bob Hope distribute a record $867,693 raised from the Bob Hope Desert Classic in 1977 to 34 local charities. *Courtesy Palm Springs Historical Society*

LEFT BOTTOM Joan and John Sinn, Bob Hope, Barbara and Vice President George Bush, Betty and Gerald Ford, Dolores Hope and Eleanor and Leonard Firestone attend the dedication of the Betty Ford Center at Eisenhower Medical Center, Oct. 3, 1981. *Courtesy Bob Hope Classic archives*

OPPOSITE: Aerial view of Eisenhower Medical Center, circa 1995. *Courtesy Bob Hope Classic archives*

ABOVE: Arnold Palmer's fifth Classic title came in 1973 when he edged out Jack Nicklaus and Johnny Miller on a rainy afternoon at Bermuda Dunes Country Club. *Courtesy Bob Hope Classic archives*

OPPOSITE BOTTOM: Famed for its traditional perfect so-called "Hope Weather," the Classic did occasionally have a few soggy days. Here, Jack Nicklaus tees off on the first hole of La Quinta County Club in 1973. *Courtesy Desert Sun archives*

The King of the Desert

·····································

The morning of Feb. 11, 1973, broke with a cold rain lightly falling on Bermuda Dunes Country Club.

The uncharacteristic gray sky showed only occasional signs of yielding for the sun, and the rain would pelt the golf course sporadically throughout the day.

It would be one of the worst days of weather in the 14 years of Bob Hope's tournament, but it would also provide a fitting setting for perhaps the most dramatic day of golf in the event's history.

Jack Nicklaus, already considered by some as the sport's best golfer, was ready to clash with his friend, business partner and rival, Arnold Palmer. It was a final-pairing match-up golf fans had seen repeatedly since the 1962 U.S. Open. That's when the upstart Nicklaus defeated his older foe in an 18-hole playoff in Palmer's backyard of Oakmont Country Club near Pittsburgh.

On this day, Nicklaus, the Golden Bear, would try to hold off Palmer, the undisputed king of the game who had ruled the Hope since 1960.

"I remember John Schlee (the third man in the final group that day) walking onto the first tee and saying to me, 'I've come along to referee this match,'" Palmer recalled.

The fans at Bermuda Dunes that day broke out rain coats and umbrellas to protect themselves from the unusual weather. They also did what most golf fans had done for the past 15 years – unabashedly throw their support behind Palmer.

While a pro-Palmer sentiment was a sure thing at almost any stop on the PGA Tour, it was even stronger in the desert. That's where Palmer, then 43, had won five previous times, including four Hope titles. Palmer even stayed at Bermuda Dunes whenever he was in the desert.

By day's end, the fans were rewarded with a stirring battle that saw neither player gain a clear advantage most of the day. Palmer beat Nicklaus and emerging star Johnny Miller by two shots. The victory snapped a two-year winless drought for Palmer stretching back to the 1971 Hope.

But Palmer had done more than just win a tournament, a victory that turned out to be his last on the tour. He also added to his stature as the most charismatic figure in the history of the Desert Classic.

In many ways, Hope's tournament had belonged to Palmer even more than to the comedian. Palmer won it twice before Hope agreed to lend his name to the event.

The love affair between Palmer and the desert began four years before Hope's tournament debuted in 1960. Palmer, a promising young pro with a growing reputation for aggressive play and a powerful swing, came to the Coachella Valley for the 1956 Thunderbird Invitational. He had been a pro just over a year.

"I missed the first year I was a pro (1955)," Palmer recalled. "I didn't get an invitation to the Thunderbird because I had no record. The only thing I had was the Amateur Championship (in 1954). That was my exemption to the tour."

Palmer had still come to the desert in 1955 with his wife, Winnie, just to get to know the area.

It was about that time that Hope first saw Palmer

ABOVE: Johnny Miller, Bob Hope, Andy Williams and Cary Middlecoff, 1973. *Courtesy Bob Hope Classic archives*

RIGHT: A classic pose of Arnold Palmer's powerful and unique follow-through that dominated not only the early days of the Classic, but the entire PGA tour.
Courtesy Desert Sun archives

BELOW: Arnold Palmer cranks up his powerful swing on the driving range during the 1962 Classic that he won.
Courtesy Bob Hope Classic archives

during a pro-am round at the Los Angeles Open. Like most people seeing Palmer for the first time, Hope was awed by the raw power of the muscular young man, the result of a unique blocked follow-through and long shots of low trajectory.

Hope joked that when Palmer swung the club, the earth shook.

By the time he came to the desert in January 1956, Palmer had earned his first pro win at the 1955 Canadian Open. Palmer was mostly an eastern player at the time, a Pennsylvania native who played college golf at Wake Forest in North Carolina. But, Palmer took an immediate liking to the desert.

"I had a lot of good tournaments here. I liked the conditions. I liked the golf courses. They were all very well-manicured, and the weather was usually nice and warm," Palmer said.

Palmer never threatened to win the 1956 event at Thunderbird Country Club, finishing 10 shots behind winner Jimmy Demaret. But a final-round 67 pushed Palmer into a tie for sixth and earned him his first check in Palm Springs: $365.

Beyond the sun-splashed weather and beautiful courses, Palmer discovered friends and kindred spirits in the desert. One was Jim Vickers, who had played college golf against Palmer when Palmer was at Wake Forest and Vickers was at Oklahoma.

"I played against Arnold in the East-West matches in the 1950 Intercollegiate at Albuquerque," Vickers said. "We've been friends ever since."

Palmer returned to the Thunderbird in 1957 but skipped the event in 1958. That year he won his first major championship at the Masters and led the tour in earnings for the first time.

When the 29-year-old Palmer returned to Thunderbird in 1959, he was becoming a big star in a game that saw many of its top players – Ben Hogan, Sam Snead and Demaret, for example – nearing their 50th birthdays.

Palmer stole the show at the 1959 Thunderbird in what would become expected form for him.

Trailing Demaret by five shots starting the final round, Palmer shot a 30 on the front nine, then came home in 32 for a 10-under 62. His 22-under 266 total was three shots better than Demaret, a three-time Thunderbird winner, and Ken Venturi, the event's defending champion.

The 266 broke the tournament record by two shots, and the 62 was just one shot off the course record set by Bo Wininger.

"That's a win a lot of people forget about," Palmer said. "They think about the five wins in what would be Bob's tournament, but the one at Thunderbird counts, too."

The Thunderbird title, the 11th in just over three years for Palmer, would be one he would not officially defend. By 1960, the tournament had folded, a victim of an unacceptably low $15,000 purse and waning interest among Thunderbird members.

For 1960, the tournament was transformed into the Palm Springs Classic, a 90-hole, four-course, five-day event.

The change made little difference to Palmer. However, it was another Palmer, popular pro Johnny Palmer, who led the 1960 event after 72 holes. The final round was scheduled for the same Thunderbird course Arnold Palmer had scorched in 1959, and the results were almost the same.

This time, Arnold Palmer finished with a 65 for a three-shot win over Fred Hawkins.

Hope's initial impression of Palmer was right. When Palmer swung, the earth did move, literally and figuratively. Palmer was fast becoming not just the biggest name in golf but a figure that transcended the game.

Hope, always determined to find people and material to keep his act fresh and relevant, previously arranged for golfers like Demaret and Hogan to appear on his TV shows. Now, it was Palmer's turn.

"I did his show (and) I did a movie in 1961 with him," Palmer said. "Hope was a friend of a lot of the older guys even before I came upon the scene, and he played in the Crosby. Bob Hope was always an avid golfer and spent a great deal of time with the game. We became pretty good friends."

Palmer's motion picture debut came in a typical Hope film of the time called "Call Me Bwana." Filmed in England, Palmer's part somehow failed to inspire a Best Supporting Actor nomination.

The entire scene consisted of Hope having breakfast in a tent in the desert, only to discover his hard-boiled egg was really a golf ball. Palmer stepped into the tent, surveyed the ball, then hit a shot out of the tent flap as a befuddled Hope looked on.

When he appeared on Hope's TV specials, Palmer filled the role that many other stars had filled. Hope intentionally would set himself up as the butt of the jokes, allowing the guest to get the laughs while Hope gave a deadpan look to the audience.

"The last time I saw you you were in Palm Springs winning the desert Classic, and now you are here on my show," Hope would say.

"Well, you win some, you lose some," Palmer replied, drawing laughs from the audience.

"Call Me Bwana" failed to change Palmer's career choice. But it did continue his ascent as a media personality that golf had not seen since the height of Bobby Jones' career.

Palmer's explosive 1960 season, including his Classic win, came about the same time television was discovering the game. Palmer was a perfect leading man for TV, powerful and good looking with a blue-collar work ethic and flair for pulling off high-risk shots and rallying for dramatic wins. He was Errol Flynn in spikes, slashing his way to victory not with a sword but with a 9-iron.

Hope was far from the only celebrity Palmer became

friendly with through the Classic or old Thunderbird tournament. Palmer tells the story of walking through the clubhouse on the way to a round and receiving good luck wishes from band leader and Jack Benny sidekick Phil Harris.

Palmer saw how celebrities like Crosby and Hope had helped the professional game, and he lobbied for more celebrities to get involved with tournaments.

"I tried to help that a little bit by talking to people like Hope and getting them interested because it drew attention to the tournaments," Palmer said. "I thought that was part of building the interest in golf. And it worked. It worked very well."

Palmer also tried to encourage other golfers to play in the desert. While few players skipped tournaments in the early 1960s, there were a few who wouldn't come to the desert because of concerns over the unique four-course, five-day format.

But with celebrities like Hope, Harris and Desi Arnaz in the field and generally perfect weather, the Hope became a popular stop.

"I think they all enjoyed it, the guys who came," Palmer said. "I think it took a little while for that really to take effect. But as the years went on, everyone came and played."

Palmer's influence wouldn't have been possible without stellar play on the course, and he provided plenty of that in the desert and around the rest of the country. The 1960 Palm Springs win started what was arguably the greatest year in Palmer's career.

By season's end, Palmer added seven more wins, including a second green jacket at the Masters. He also provided the single most identifiable moment of his career at the 1960 U.S. Open at Cherry Hills Country Club in Denver. Seven shots behind leader Mike Souchack, Palmer drove the green on the first hole of the final round, made birdie and went on to shoot 65 to win the Open by two shots.

Palmer won $75,263 in 1960, leading the tour in

BELOW: Arnold Palmer kisses his prize check as Desi Arnaz looks on, circa 1962. *Courtesy Bob Hope Classic archives*

ABOVE: Part of Palmer's appeal to the galleries was his willingness to show his emotions, like the concern he shows here, circa 1960s.
Courtesy Bob Hope Classic archives

LEFT: Arnold Palmer, already a tournament legend by the late 1960s, shares a moment with band leader Lawrence Welk and Hope board member John Curci, a co-owner of Indian Wells Country Club. *Courtesy Bob Hope Classic archives*

earnings for the second time in three years. By the time he came back to Palm Springs in 1961, he was the undisputed ruler of the game. He finished third in the desert that year.

When the 1962 event rolled around, however, Palmer found himself in a rare slump. He had won five tour events in 1961 and added his first British Open title. But he hadn't won since that British Open victory at Royal Birkdale in July 1961.

It had not gone unnoticed by PGA Tour officials. Someone alerted Palmer just before the Palm Springs event that he was just 22nd on the money list entering the week.

Palmer, whose competitive fires only were stoked by such observations, roared into high gear in the next five rounds. Through 72 holes, Palmer had positioned himself three shots behind leader Gene Littler, the reigning U.S. Open champion.

Palmer started the final 18 holes at Bermuda Dunes slowly, taking a bogey at the second hole to fall four behind Littler. Starting at the fifth hole, though, Palmer steamed ahead. By the end of the front nine, Palmer had made five consecutive birdies, shot 32 on the side and turned the deficit into a lead.

Littler wilted in the face of Palmer's comeback and lost by six strokes.

Again, the Palm Springs win was the catalyst for a huge year for Palmer. This time, Palmer won seven tournaments, including a third Masters, a second British Open and a third money title in five years. Palmer also lost the famous playoff at the U.S. Open to Nicklaus at Oakmont Country Club.

Indeed, Palmer's hold on the desert was rivaled only by a pair of entertainment giants, Hope and Frank Sinatra. A visit by Palmer in the early days of the Hope tournament was like a visit from royalty, complete with entourage and fawning fans.

"I would say Arnold's popularity here exceeded anywhere else," said longtime tournament board member Paul Jenkins. "But if it did, he was a benevolent king. He was wonderful to people and the gallery and always said good things in the press about the tournament."

By 1968, Palmer had earned a third Hope victory and nearly a fourth. The 1966 Hope produced the tournament's third playoff in four years, and the first to feature Palmer.

This time it was Palmer who was the victim of a final-round comeback. Doug Sanders, who had finished second in the 1961 event, fired a 66 at Indian Wells to catch Palmer, who managed just 70.

Phil Rogers eventually tied for third, one shot out of the playoff. Palmer had a chance to avoid the playoff entirely but twice in the closing holes missed easy birdie putts that could have clinched the title. One of the shots was a five-footer on the last hole that could be blamed on Palmer being too popular with the fans.

As Palmer stood over the putt, fans scrambled up the rocky mountainside just behind the 18th green to get a glimpse of their hero. They inadvertently started a small rockslide, and Palmer was forced to back off the putt twice before missing.

Instead of another Palmer win, the duo went to a playoff that Sanders won.

"To beat Arnold, well, that was something," Sanders said.

Palmer finished a mere 32nd in the 1967 Classic, 13 shots behind surprise winner Tom Nieporte, a club pro at Winged Foot Country Club in New York and only a part-time tour player..

The next year, Palmer fell out of the top-10 money winners on tour for the first time since 1956. But his magic at the Hope continued, this time with Palmer winning a playoff.

Despite 10 top-10 finishes in the 1970 season, the 1971 West Coast swing began with Palmer badly needing a win. What better place to break the slump than in the desert of Palm Springs, and particularly in a year when the Classic was to be hosted by Bermuda Dunes, the site of two of Palmer's previous three Hope wins and where Palmer had a condo?

For the first four rounds, Palmer was on a mission. He finished 72 holes in 16 under par, including a third-round 66, to grab a three-shot lead over Bert Yancey and Raymond Floyd.

In a normal tournament, Palmer's victory drought would be over. In the Hope, he had 18 more holes to play.

The win ultimately came, as Palmer edged Floyd in a playoff.

As exciting as the playoff was for the gallery, the trophy presentation caused even more of a stir. Just as Palmer was receiving the trophy, a man charged him and the gathered dignitaries on the 18th green. The man, later identified as a caddie fired by Orville Moody during the week for "excessive drinking," was screaming charges that the tournament had been rigged.

ABOVE: Deane Beman being interviewed by Dr. Cary Middlecoff after Arnold beat Beman in the playoff in 1968. Beman went on to become the commissioner of the PGA Tour. *Courtesy Bob Hope Classic archives*

LEFT: Arnold Palmer became the first three-time winner of the Classic with a 1968 playoff win over Deane Beman. Here, Palmer discusses the victory with reporters. *Courtesy Bob Hope Classic archives*

While it's a bad idea to break through security screaming at a golf tournament, it's a particularly bad idea when the vice president of the United States, complete with Secret Service protection, is handing that award to the winner.

The disgruntled ex-caddie never got close to Palmer, Hope or Vice President Spiro Agnew and was literally carried off the course by Secret Service agents to a waiting police car.

Palmer, for one, couldn't understand what the man was talking about.

"He didn't get to me, but he was yelling something about the tournament being fixed," Palmer said after the ceremony. "Fixed, huh? I wish they had told me about it being fixed when I teed off this morning."

As exciting as Palmer's three playoffs in the Hope had been, nothing matched the sheer drama of his 1973 win, a two-shot victory over Nicklaus and Miller. It was the ultimate tournament for the golf fan: Palmer, the veteran warrior at 43, playing in the final group of the day with Nicklaus, the man who had stolen Palmer's crown in the 1962 U.S. Open.

Little did anyone know it would be Palmer's last winning moment on the PGA Tour.

It was also the only time the game's two biggest names squared off in the Hope. The only other time they both finished in the top 10 in the tournament was in 1963, when Nicklaus beat Player in a playoff while Palmer finished sixth.

While Palmer played the Hope every year, Nicklaus had skipped four of the previous 11 events. Nicklaus had

LEFT: Arnold Palmer and Jack Nicklaus at Indian Wells in 1967. *Courtesy Bob Hope Classic archives*

OPPOSITE: A couple of longtime golfing buddies Arnold Palmer and Bob Hope striking a familiar pose on the golf course. *Courtesy Desert Sun archives*

played in 1962 and 1968, years of Palmer victories, but wasn't in the field when Palmer won in 1971. Nicklaus wasn't wild about the tournament format and then began shaping his schedules around major championships.

Things didn't look promising early for Palmer supporters in the 1973 event, as Nicklaus shot a 64 in the first round to take the lead while Palmer opened with a tepid 71.

Nicklaus shared the third-round lead with Allen Miller after a 71, while Palmer continued to creep up with a 69 and was now just one shot back. After 72 holes, it was Johnny Miller, who set a course record with a 63 at Tamarisk, who

had tied Nicklaus. Palmer was one shot back.

This battle was pitched from the first hole, a 531-yard par-5. Palmer electrified the crowd with a birdie, while Nicklaus struggled to a bogey. For the first time in the tournament, it was Palmer's name on top of the leader board.

For the rest of the day, it was the Bear chasing the King, with Palmer maintaining a lead of one or two shots. At the par-4 16th, it appeared Nicklaus had his chance to reverse the damage from the first hole. Palmer, leading by two shots, found a bunker on his second shot, and Nicklaus hit his approach just three feet from the cup.

BELOW: Even past his competitive prime, Arnold Palmer still drew some of the largest galleries in golf like this picture of his "army" keeping pace with the King in 1985. *Courtesy Desert Sun archives*

Palmer, though, recovered to save his par. Then Nicklaus, perhaps the greatest clutch putter in the game's history, stunningly missed his birdie putt. Palmer had escaped another threat.

Nicklaus had one final chance. On the 501-yard par-5 closing hole, he powered his second shot onto the green, setting up a potential eagle. Palmer's 3-wood second shot came up just short of the massive green, leaving him a testy chip.

The chip rolled three feet past the cup, the same length that Nicklaus had missed just two holes earlier.

Nicklaus studied the putt and then stood over it for what seemed like an eternity to the pro-Palmer gallery. It was a habit that dogged Nicklaus' entire career.

"The only thing that was wrong with Jack was we always thought, 'Would he ever hit the putt?'" Dolores Hope said. "But he was always such a nice person."

Nicklaus' 20-footer seemed true until the last instant, when it veered slightly right and missed the cup. He was left with a tap-in birdie, but Palmer was now just two putts from his 62nd career win.

There would be no two-putt for Palmer, though, who drained his putt for a birdie and one of the most satisfying

victories in his career. He had defeated the rain, Nicklaus and the ghosts of a 24-month winless streak.

Palmer's relief and excitement were evident. Smiling broadly, he hurled his visor high into the air and virtually sprinted off the green to be greeted by handshakes and a quick hug from Nicklaus.

Palmer would never again win a PGA Tour event, and he would never finish higher than 20th in the Hope. Yet, he remained the tournament's strongest drawing card among the pros and even outdrew many of the celebrities who populated the tournament.

The Classic even intertwined with Palmer's personal life. The only time Palmer failed to play at least 72 holes in a Hope that he started was in 1976. As he walked off the course after the third round, Palmer was informed by Dunlevie that Palmer's father, Deacon Palmer, had died of a massive heart attack that morning. Palmer withdrew and flew back to Bay Hill, Fla., where his father had played golf that morning.

While Palmer didn't complete the 1976 event, he did start the tournament, keeping alive a streak of consecutive Hope appearances that would eventually reach 37 years. Palmer had planned on making it 38

ABOVE: Arnold Palmer accepting the plaque from Jerry Hall as the first inductee into the Indian Wells Classic Hall of Fame in 1985. *Courtesy Desert Sun archives*

LEFT: Bob Hope and Arnold Palmer laugh at one of Hope's comments during the 1995 Indian Wells Country Club Hall of Fame Dinner. *Courtesy Desert Sun archives*

straight Hopes in 1997, but he had to withdraw from the tournament before even showing up to the desert.

One week before the Hope, Palmer announced that he had prostate cancer. As the rest of the tour moved from the Mercedes Championship in Carlsbad, Calif., to the Coachella Valley, Palmer flew to the Mayo Clinic in Minnesota. His surgery took place on the same day as the first round of the Hope and was immediately deemed a success by surgeons.

Palmer was playing tournament golf again just two months later, but his Hope streak was over. He returned again in 1998, and his streak eventually reached 42 of 43 tournaments through the 2002 event, even though he had not made a cut since 1981.

Palmer felt obliged to keep coming to the tournament where he had much success and fun, and the Hope

board of directors continued to beg Palmer to play even when he repeatedly said he wouldn't return after missing another Hope cut.

His last dash of magic at the Hope came in 2001 when Palmer was 71 years old.

He and his fans were disappointed with scores of 81, 77 and 75 in the first three rounds that year.

But in the fourth round, playing on the PGA West course he designed, Palmer became the story of the day. Palmer worked his way to 2 under through 15 holes, putting him in position to shoot his age on the par-72 course.

A wayward drive on the short par-4 16th found water, though, and the resulting double-bogey 6 knocked Palmer back to even par on the day.

"I was very aware that I was going to be somewhere around my age when I came in," Palmer told reporters after the round. "When I made the double bogey, I knew the last two holes and I knew there was a pretty good chance I could make a birdie on one of them."

Indeed, as the crowds following Palmer swelled, he hit a solid tee shot on the par-3 17th and made the 12-foot putt for birdie to get back to 1 under.

As Palmer played the final hole, the gallery was peppered with fans who had watched the King since his winning days of the 1960s. Some even had badges proudly proclaiming. "I'm part of Arnie's Army," badges that were older than the fans' grandchildren.

Palmer played the par-5 hole in textbook fashion and closed with a par and 71. The crowd cheered wildly, and Palmer accepted congratulations from his playing partners. It could have been 1960 all over again.

"That's what's so wonderful about him," Dolores Hope said of Palmer's annual return to the desert. "Have we honored him enough? I don't think we have."

As it turned out, Palmer's days of influence in the Hope tournament weren't quite over. ■

BELOW: Arnold Palmer and radio personality Rush Limbaugh in 2001. *Courtesy Desert Sun archives*

Jammin' in Palm Springs

*I*f there was one moment frozen in time, one lasting image that defined the early days of Bob Hope's tournament, it's a photo taken during the 1973 incarnation of a loosely run and legendary party known as the Jam Session.

It is a picture of a smiling Arnold Palmer dancing with a man sporting a blond wig jammed onto his head. Palmer's dancing partner that night was Jack Nicklaus.

"That's the year I beat Jack," Palmer says of the classic photo. "After we were finished, I said, 'What are you going to do?', and he said, 'I don't know,' so I said, 'Well come on over, have some fun. Come over to Indian Wells and join the gang and have a few drinks.' So, he agreed to do that."

Palmer was a late arrival that night at the Jam Session, which had become the most popular extracurricular activity of the Hope tournament and perhaps of the entire professional tour. When he walked into the small clubhouse at Indian Wells Country Club, the crowd was overflowing as it had been for nearly a decade as the greatest party on the PGA Tour circuit.

"I bumped into some lady, very unintentionally, a good-looking gal, and I knocked her wig off," Palmer said. "And she had her hair in curlers. Well, she was embarrassed, but I was really embarrassed. Well, I immediately thought I've got to get the attention away from her. So I picked up the wig and put it on my head."

The crowd responded with belly laughs to the sight of Palmer in the wig. One particularly loud laugh came from across the room, where Nicklaus was so amused he blew Palmer a kiss.

"Since he threw me a kiss, I said, 'Well, come on, we'll dance,'" Palmer said. "And he came over. And as soon as he got to the dance floor, I took the wig off and put it on him and put my arms around him. It was a riot. Everyone just went crazy laughing. Of course, a few drinks helped."

Chances are good that Palmer and Nicklaus wouldn't dance with each other at any other tournament on tour. But somehow at the Hope, and particularly at the Jam Session, it made perfect sense.

From even its earliest days as the Palm Springs Golf Classic, the Hope had been more than just a golf tournament. There was a culture of fun and camaraderie between the pros and amateurs, and there always seemed to be a party lurking somewhere. The biggest, most raucous and famous of those parties was the Indian Wells Jam Session.

"It was the very heart of this tournament," said amateur player Jim Crooker, also a long-time member at Indian Wells. "If you are going to say what is the difference between this and other pro-ams, well, first you've got four days. But the key to this tournament was the Jam Session. I mean, life revolved around this thing."

Palmer agreed: "That was probably one of the most fascinating and fun things about playing here. And that's not bull. It was just fun."

A party on tour in the 1960s or early 1970s wasn't exactly news. After all, the image of the professional golfer in the late 1950s and into the 1960s was not one of the well-toned, muscular athlete who starts off each day with a protein shake and 100 push-ups.

More likely, the men battling for the trophy each Sunday were chain smokers who didn't shy away from an after-round drink or late hours that sometimes threatened their ability to make the next day's tee time. Players drove to tournaments when they were close enough, often with three or four in a car. Hotels were often little more than flop houses for the week.

Naturally, the tour developed a bit of a reputation

ABOVE: Desi Arnaz performs at one of the earliest Jam Sessions at Indian Wells Country Club, a club he helped found. *Courtesy Bob Hope Classic archives*

as a floating cocktail party interrupted by rounds of golf. Some players lived the high life better than others. Perhaps the most famous was three-time Masters champion Jimmy Demaret.

The charismatic Houston native dressed unlike any pro before, searching out a rainbow of colors and variety of fabrics for his wildly entertaining outfits, years before Doug Sanders strutted his peacock colors.

But Demaret's clothes weren't the only thing wild about the Texan. He could stand toe to toe with Ben Hogan and Sam Snead on the course, outdrink Phil Harris at the bar and outduel Bob Hope in a battle of one-liners.

Demaret was inducted into the World Golf Hall of Fame in 1983, the same year as Hope's entry. He admitted after his career that he could have won more tournaments if he'd been able to clear his vision on Sunday mornings after some long, long Saturday nights.

No one can say for sure if it was a late night at the Jam Session or just a case of 53-year-old nerves that were the cause of Demaret's near-miss in the 1964 Classic.

Demaret was no stranger to success in the desert, having won three times in the old Thunderbird pro-am, the tournament that preceded the Classic. But Demaret hadn't won on tour since 1957, when he won three times.

Surrounded by his show-business friends in the pro-am of the 1964 Classic, Demaret played wonderful golf for four days and trailed leaders Billy Casper and Chuck Courtney by three shots entering the final round at Eldorado Country Club.

Casper, Courtney and others like Bob Charles and pioneering African-American pro Charlie Sifford faded in the final round. But Demaret continued his steady play to stay ahead of talented Tommy Jacobs, who also was a touring pro at Classic course Bermuda Dunes.

Demaret seemed poised for a dramatic and wildly popular win as he reached the par-4 17th with a one-shot lead. But Demaret's putting suddenly fell apart, and he three-putted from 18 feet for a bogey-5. The dropped

shot put Demaret into a playoff with Jacobs.

Demaret's second chance at the win came on the first hole of the playoff, the par-5 first hole. Jacobs' drive landed behind a tree in the rough, and he was only able to pitch out and eventually hit the green in four. After a poor drive onto an undeveloped housing pad to the left of the fairway, Demaret recovered and found the green in three.

He then lagged his first putt to about two feet from the cup. Jacobs, already in with a 6, watched as Demaret took what seemed like forever to hit the short putt.

To the shock and disappointment of most of the gallery, Demaret missed the putt. Disheartened he marched off to the par-3 second hole, where he hit his tee shot into the gallery. Jacobs won the title with a routine par.

In typical Demaret fashion, the loser had a laugh in defeat.

"Tommy's a good boy," Demaret said of Jacobs, 24 years his junior. "I've got a lot of years left, and he's just about through."

Demaret played in the Classic just once more, in 1965, withdrawing after two rounds. But it's safe to say in his six years in the Classic, Demaret and other pros appreciated how the Hope and Jam Session elevated the blending of professional golf and night life to an art form.

For each night of the tournament, one of the smallest clubhouses in the desert at Indian Wells Country Club would unite tour players, amateurs, world-famous celebrities, world-class entertainment and a liberal amount of adult libations. The result: the classiest and most sought-after party on tour.

"The spectators that would come down for the tournament would kill to get in that room,"

said pro Bob Rosburg.

Imagine Gary Player belting out a few songs for the crowd ("Gary had a pretty good voice, actually," Palmer recalled), followed by Demaret or Desi Arnaz.

Imagine movie musical star Donald O'Connor whirling across the stage while U.S. Open champion Ken Venturi kept a beat on the drums, all for the amusement of a crowd that included former President Dwight Eisenhower and his wife, Mamie.

It all happened several times during each Hope tournament at the Jam Session.

Credit for the Jam Session falls, in all likelihood, to Eddie Susalla.

He was at Indian Wells from its beginning in 1956, having come to the course from an assistant pro job at nearby Thunderbird Country Club. Susalla designed the Indian Wells course and was the club's general manager when the Palm Springs tournament began in 1960.

Susalla wanted to arrange some kind of show or entertainment to keep golfers in the tournament from leaving Indian Wells at the end of the round. The answer was an intimate party with a small musical group headed by another important figure in the evolution of the Jam Session, Murray Arnold.

Arnold was a popular lounge act in Las Vegas who played the Skyline Room at the Desert Inn Country Club. He had met many of the celebrities in Las Vegas, and the golfers at the old Tournament of Champions played at the Desert Inn. Arnold would also show up at other tournaments to play, but it was the way he orchestrated the Jam Session that made him a fixture at the Hope.

Arnold's skill at the piano and familiarity with the worlds of golf and Hollywood helped jump-start the parties. Susalla's plan worked as golfers began hanging around the Indian Wells clubhouse to hear Arnold's group.

At Arnold's urging, a few of his famous friends would take the stage. As the party wore on, Arnold didn't need to urge anyone to come up. Instead, there was

competition to get a few minutes on stage.

A typical Jam Sessions evening would begin around 4:30 p.m., once play in the tournament was over for the day at all four courses. Golfers would rush to Indian Wells, where the clubhouse had been divided into two sections.

The dining room was for the players, amateurs and celebrities. The bar was roped off for gallery members with clubhouse badges. It was standing-room only on both sides of the rope.

In the dining room, large 12-foot round tables were set up, each capable of seating 15 to 18 people. Each table was reserved, with the same players and amateurs often sitting at the same table annually.

Each table was stocked with full bottles of scotch, vodka, bourbon and wine. In the early days of the Jam Session, the club had tried to have waitresses deliver drinks to each table, but the room was too crowded and the patrons found the wait too long. So each table became a kind of no-host bar.

On stage would be Murray Arnold, with maybe a bass player and guitarist just to provide a little background music as the crowd gathered. But Arnold's trio would grow as the players showed up.

As soon as Venturi walked in, he'd head to the stage and take his place at the drums.

"Murray Arnold had the trio, so I didn't bring any drums," Venturi said. "I play drums. It's like the guy who says I play golf. I shoot 95, (and) I play golf. Well, I played drums. What are we talking about? Compared to Gene Krupa, I'm a 25 handicapper."

Venturi was hardly the only golfer who fancied himself an entertainer worthy of some stage time. Former PGA Championship winner Lionel Hebert would stroll in and join the group on trumpet. Actor Buddy Rogers would produce a trombone and form a shaky horn section with Hebert.

Naturally, the group needed a conductor, and that generally fell to Palmer.

As the music played on, there was no shortage of vocal accompaniment. Arnaz might start the evening off, but he would soon give way to others.

Demaret, who sang on a few of Hope's television shows, would sing a song or two, as would Gary Player when he was in the tournament.

In between their turns at the microphone, people who actually sang for a living would get up and perform.

Another mainstay was Don Cherry, a fine amateur golfer in his day who lost to Palmer in the 1954 U.S. Amateur. Cherry had a terrific voice and even had some minor hits as a singer.

The Jam Session was the perfect blend of an audience for Cherry. There were pro golfers he had competed against, entertainment celebrities who knew Cherry as a singer and amateur golfers who were just star-struck enough to see Cherry as a viable star in the golf and entertainment world.

If the pros and celebrities weren't on stage, they were competing for laughs and drinks in the audience.

"It was an endurance contest, really," Crooker said.

Palmer and Nicklaus were hardly the only golfers to hit the dance floor.

"The people we would have would go from Arnold right down through to Jack," Susalla said. "You wouldn't normally see Jack getting up and dancing at some place like that. Even Gene Littler would be in there dancing, and that's the fastest he'd moved in a long time. Miller Barber and some of the guys who you look at them today, you wouldn't think they ever danced."

It might all seem a bit unseemly by today's standards, world-class professional golfers dancing, drinking and partying several times during tournament week with amateurs and celebrities. But those who were part of the Jam Sessions staunchly support the parties as a creature of the times and just a harmless good time.

"No one was smoking pot or anything like that," Susalla said. "People were just having fun, and it was something different. Maybe it was the atmosphere,

maybe it was just the closeness of the people. They weren't as goofy as the ones running around today. You just walked in and you had to know someone, and it would just start building from that. And no one would want to leave."

The parties rolled on into the mid-1970s. But slowly, the Jam Sessions began to die, though everyone has a different reason for the end.

For Rosburg, the end began when the attitudes of the players and even PGA Tour officials changed toward the event.

"I think the thing that happened with the Jam Session is that the players stopped going. And I think that killed it," Rosburg said. "It became a thing that you shouldn't do. And that was all (Commissioner Deane) Beman."

Beman took over as commissioner of the tour in 1974, six years after losing the Hope tournament in a playoff to Palmer. The start of Beman's 21-year reign as commissioner was also about the time the Jam Sessions began to slow down. Rosburg said he believes the conservative, image-conscious Beman let it be known that he wasn't happy with the idea of his players dancing and drinking the night away after a competitive round.

"He thought it was not professional," Rosburg said.

For Crooker, the end was signaled when the celebrities in the tournament no longer clamored to hit the stage. Much of the spontaneity also dissipated.

Another significant reason for the demise of the Jam Sessions was the pros themselves. As the tournament moved

into the 1970s, fewer and fewer players with ties to the 1950s were playing the tour.

The players from that decade were more likely to have been brought into the game first as caddies, then later as club professionals whose business it was to play with and often socialize with amateurs. That would carry through to their days on the tour, which were often still sandwiched in between club jobs.

"You used to go in and play gin with the members, have a few drinks when you came in," Rosburg said.

By the 1970s, the older tour pros were being replaced by a generation of younger golfers who honed their skills in college golf tournaments – not at the driving range after a day's work in the pro shop. The modern players weren't necessarily any less friendly, but they certainly hadn't been ingrained with the idea of rubbing shoulders and sharing drinks with amateur players.

Perhaps the most significant change was the burgeoning size of tour purses.

In 1960, total purses for the entire tour stood at just over $1.3 million. By 1970, that figure was $6.7 million, and by 1980 it was $13.4 million.

As the purses grew, so, too, did the players' desire to earn their share of the money. That meant staying in shape and not staying out as much as players had a generation earlier.

"Now think about it," Crooker said. "When the guys are finished, they are out there hitting balls or whatever. I'd make a comment after a round like, 'I can't wait to get to the bar.' And the pro that was playing with us started saying, 'Well, I'm going to hit the range.'

"They replaced the Jam Session with fitness trailers." ∎

LEFT: Two Arnolds, Arnold Palmer, left, and Murray Arnold, share a laugh at the Jam Session in 1972. Murray Arnold was in charge of coordinating music for the event each year. *Courtesy Bob Hope Classic archives*

TOP: During the 1973 Jam Session, a "blonde" Arnold Palmer shares a laugh – maybe even a dance – with Jack Nicklaus. It was one of the most memorable moments from the storied chapter of Jam Sessions at the Bob Hope Chrysler Classic over the years. *Courtesy Arnold Palmer Enterprises*

Bob and Jerry

New Haven, Conn., in the 1930s was a popular stop on the circuit for theatrical shows and reviews on their way to or from Broadway.

Shows looking to add a song, cut a scene or just sharpen the material of a comedy act would stop in New Haven, among other northeastern cities, to try out the changes for eager audiences who might never get to New York City to see the show in its final form.

Shows that had played out in New York would hit the road to squeeze out a few more dollars for the producers.

The beneficiaries of the shows in New Haven were often the students at the town's most famous institution, Yale University. It was Yale's highly respected law school that had attracted a young aspiring lawyer from Grand Rapids, Mich., named Gerald Ford.

One night in 1937, Ford attended a review show called "Red, Hot and Blue," at the Taft Theater. The show featured three of the biggest stars of the day: Ethel Merman, Jimmy Durante and Bob Hope.

"A friend of mine said he knew Bob and so we went to the show," recalled Ford, in an interview before his 2006 death in the desert.

He eventually went backstage with the friend. "Afterwards, we had a cup of coffee with Bob and Dolores."

Ford couldn't have known that the backstage meeting with Hope was the first encounter in what would become a long, close friendship that would blossom decades later from that 1937 evening.

Simultaneously, Hope couldn't have possibly known he was having a casual cup of coffee with a future president of the United States.

Thirty-eight years after that first meeting, and just 20 days after he left the White House in 1977, Ford became one of the main characters in Hope's PGA Tour event in the Southern California desert.

Ford remained a constant in his friend's tournament for the next 21 years, knocking a few shots into the galleries and gladly suffering the barbs of Hope and other comedians in the name of his friendship with Hope and the good of Ford's adopted desert home.

By playing at Hope's side, Ford added a new twist to an already multidimensional pro-am tournament.

Hope was the ringmaster and the clown, the center of attention who kept things light and entertaining.

Arnold Palmer's role was of the dashing leading man, giving the gallery a rooting interest and keeping them riveted to the leader board even when fans knew Palmer was past his winning days.

Ford became the elder statesman of the event. He brought the dignity and legitimacy of a man who had been a trusted public servant for three more decades, who had risen beyond his aspirations to become president in the most difficult scenario of America's modern history.

But Ford also brought a touch of the common man to the event, at least as common as any former resident of the White House could be. He sprayed the ball around the golf course, seemed intimidated by the galleries and in awe of some of the game's biggest names.

"He was the former president of the United States and people wanted to get up close to him," Hope board member Ernie Dunlevie said. "They wanted to see him play lousy golf just like they did."

Ford's commitment to Hope's tournament in 1977 had its seeds planted in that casual meeting in New Haven 40 years before. But Ford and Hope crossed paths many times before they first played golf together in 1974, just after Ford took over the presidency.

Six years after their initial meeting in New Haven, Ford and Hope met again. This time, the globetrotting

---

RIGHT: Bob Hope and President Gerald Ford in 1985.
Courtesy Bob Hope Classic archives (bh86t011001)

comedian came to see Ford, who was serving in the U.S. Navy in the Pacific in World War II.

"Bob and his group of entertainers came through and performed at one of the atolls where we were temporarily getting re-supplied," Ford said. "Bob and his group put on a terrific show. That was a welcome break in our wartime activities. Bob did more to help the morale of the military than anyone in the history of the country."

After the war, Ford set his eyes on a private law practice in Grand Rapids and a possible run for elective office in 1948. His interest in golf, which began in his childhood in Michigan, was all but gone.

"When I was in high school or younger, I caddied for my father (actually Ford's stepfather), who was a Sunday afternoon golfer," Ford said. "But I never had time. I was always playing football or basketball. So I never really took golf seriously until I came out here (to Palm Springs)."

It was strange that as president, Ford's missteps on stairs could be wildly lampooned by comedians like Chevy Chase in his slapstick, falling-down impersonations on "Saturday Night Live." In reality, Ford was one of the most athletic men to occupy the Oval Office.

It was football in particular that occupied the young Ford and eventually helped him earn his way into the University of Michigan. Ford was an excellent student in college, but he was best known as the star center on the Wolverine football squads that went undefeated in 1932 and 1933. The Wolverines struggled to a 1-7 record in Ford's senior year, but the scrappy center was named the team's most valuable player.

Ford's football prowess attracted interest from both the Green Bay Packers and the Detroit Lions of the fledgling National Football League. But it was politics, not athletics, that was in Ford's future.

Ford had been bitten by the political bug during a trip to Washington, D.C., as a teenager. After graduating from Michigan, he chose to attend law school at Yale, where he also was an assistant coach for the football team.

Ford was eventually elected to the House of Representatives in 1948, just weeks after marrying his now equally famous wife, Betty. He represented Grand Rapids for the next 25 years.

The leadership qualities that were shaped on the football field stood out in Congress and impressed both Ford's fellow Republicans and the Democrats across the aisle. Ford was eventually elevated to the position of House minority leader, where respect for Ford continued to grow.

The demands of such a high-profile leadership position, plus the demands of four growing children, continued to keep Ford off the golf course.

In 1973, Ford's life was altered drastically when Vice President Spiro Agnew resigned after pleading no contest to tax evasion charges. President Richard Nixon, already fighting his own battles over the Watergate scandal, chose Ford to serve as the new vice president.

Just over one year later, on Aug. 9, 1974, Nixon resigned in the face of impeachment because of the Watergate affair. Ford was elevated to the presidency.

Ford held the office for just 29 months, losing a close election to Jimmy Carter in November 1976. It was while Ford occupied the White House that the country learned of his growing love for golf.

Unlike Dwight Eisenhower, who is credited with playing nearly 800 rounds of golf during his two terms in the White House, Ford managed only to sneak in a round, sometimes two, in a month. Occasionally, one of those rounds would be with Hope, one of the few civilians in the world who could make a tee time with a president.

Ford and Hope forged a solid friendship, centered on their mutual love of the sport.

When it became apparent that the Fords would be leaving the White House in January 1977 after losing the election, Ford and his wife made a critical decision that directly affected his participation in Hope's tournament.

Like thousands of other golfing retirees, the Fords decided to spend their winters near Palm Springs. The decision was actually an easy one because the Fords had been visiting the desert since his years in the House of Representatives. They were invited to Palm Springs by friends.

"When we left the White House, we looked at Florida, but it was too damp for Mrs. Ford's arthritis. We looked at Pebble Beach. Again, it was too damp and too windy," Ford said. "And we'd been coming here, we had friends here. So, with the climate and friends, it seemed a good place."

The Fords bought two home lots at Thunderbird Country Club, one for a private home and one for a suite of offices. The arrangements for the move and the

ABOVE: President Gerald Ford and defending Classic Champion Johnny Miller in 1977. *Courtesy Desert Sun archives*

OPPOSITE: President Gerald Ford and Bob Hope with the Classic girls in the late 1978. the Classic girls, from left, are Valerie McDonald, Denise Smith, and Elaine Carothers. *Courtesy Bob Hope Classic archives*

homes were all made before Ford officially left office on Jan. 20, 1977. That day, with Carter having taken the oath of office, Ford took a nostalgic helicopter tour of Washington, D.C.

He then headed off to a new life. It became apparent quite quickly what his priority would be: That very afternoon, Ford flew to Pebble Beach and managed to get in about 30 minutes on the practice range before sunset.

Ford had been invited to play in the Bing Crosby Pro-Am, where he would be paired with Arnold Palmer. The day after he left office, Ford and Palmer played in a

foursome with Hale Irwin and another amateur.

After a second round with Palmer at Crosby's tournament, Ford turned his attention to the Hope, which began just 20 days after he left the White House. Because of his friendship with Hope, it was natural that Ford would play in the Desert Classic. What few knew was that Ford nearly made history in the tournament a year earlier.

"I contemplated playing in the Bob Hope while I was in office," Ford admits. "I played in one PGA tournament (a pre-tournament pro-am) down in North Carolina when we dedicated the PGA Hall of Fame, but that was just a one-day event."

All the arrangements for Ford's visit to the Hope had been made by Ford's staff while he was still in office. Ford's appearance gave Hope officials a chance to start two new traditions. Ford would, of course, play with Hope and another celebrity.

For the 1977 tournament the celebrity was Sammy Davis Jr. The other new tradition would be for the Ford-Hope amateur team to play the first round each year with the defending champion in what the tournament dubbed the First Foursome.

It may not be a coincidence that no player managed to seriously threaten repeating as champion at the Classic while playing the first round with Hope and Ford.

Between Hope's entourage, Ford and his Secret Service protection and the crowds drawn by whoever the third amateur was, the First Foursome drew large, raucous crowds, gawkers and autograph seekers who sneaked in cameras against PGA Tour rules.

TOP LEFT: Professional golfer Lee Trevino with President Gerald Ford, 1978. *Courtesy Bob Hope Classic archives*

BOTTOM LEFT: The "First Foursome" in 1978 included President Gerald Ford, Bob Hope, professional Billy Casper and Jackie Gleason. *Courtesy Bob Hope Classic archives*

Try shooting 66 with all that going on around you.

Ford's own game had shown some rust at the Crosby, something he hoped wouldn't be evident as he began his Hope career.

"My game needed a lot of attention, and I was dedicated to working and improving my game," Ford said. "But when you are playing with Bob Hope and a top pro, there is always a big crowd from the tee to the green.

With my wildness off the tee, I was always intimidated by what was going to happen to the golf ball."

Hope loved having his friend in the tournament, particularly the 1977 event when Ford added a fresh face and national attention to the 18th annual event. As he had done with Vice President Spiro Agnew seven years earlier, Hope enjoyed the chance to keep the tournament topical while also taking a few verbal shots at Ford's game

ABOVE: President Gerald Ford speaks to the reporters after a round during the 1980 Classic.
Courtesy Bob Hope Classic archives

LEFT: Bruce Lietzke, flanked by Bob Hope and President Gerald Ford, holds the $50,000 check he earned by winning the 1981 Classic. *Courtesy Desert Sun archives*

for the benefit of the crowd.

Through the years, Ford became the No. 1 target of Hope's golf jokes. They were classic one-liners:

"You never know which golf course Ford is playing until after he hits his drive."

"Gerald Ford could lose a ball in a ball washer."

"The best way to keep track of Ford's score was just to count the number of people he hit in a round."

"You can tell Gerald Ford is improving because he's only hitting Democrats now."

Hope's own competitiveness and disdain for losing on the course often would come through in his rounds

with Ford. That meant more than just the quick jab over one of Ford's misdirected drives.

"He did worse things than that," Ford said. "More than once right in the midst of my back swing, he would make some comment. Or he might cough. He always had a slightly derogatory comment about a shot I would make."

Ford was never one to just sit back and take Hope's barbs without firing back. One of Ford's favorite comments was how Hope began entertaining the troops for Grant at Gettysburg.

Ford annually wrote a letter for the introduction of the Hope program, giving the former president another chance to mock Hope's playing ability or, more often, Hope's age.

"One time I wrote it's always nice to play with someone who played with Taft and Wilson," Ford smiled.

"I want one of two things from you," a tongue-in-cheek Ford wrote in his 1985 program letter. "Either you stop making jokes about my infrequent errant shots, or starting now, I get two shots a side when we play."

Ford later joked that he really didn't mind Hope making fun of him, because he knew Hope had treated other presidents exactly the same – presidents like Teddy Roosevelt, James Polk and Andrew Jackson.

Still, the give-and-take would eventually turn into Hope giving and Ford taking. "You all know Gerald Ford, the most dangerous driver since Ben Hur," Hope would say on the tee box.

The jabbing was all in fun, since the two families would play golf and have dinner together as often as they could.

"The Hopes and the Fords, I would say, have as good a relationship as anyone we know in the desert," Ford said.

"There are no greater two people in the world than those two," Dolores Hope said. "God bless them. It is so wonderful to know people like that and the humility of them and the niceness. It's just wonderful."

Ford annually played in the desert's other big professional tournament, the LPGA's Nabisco Dinah Shore (later the Kraft Nabisco Championship), which featured a two-day pro-am.

Ford's presence at the Hope helped attract another famous politician to the desert. During his days in Congress and later as president, Ford had become

BELOW: Bob Hope dons a hard hat in what clearly is a joke aimed at Gerald Ford as Mickey Rooney, right, breaks up, 1987. *Courtesy Bob Hope Classic archives*

fast friends with Thomas P. "Tip" O'Neill, a Boston Democrat who eventually became Speaker of the House.

The political adversaries became golfing buddies. Throughout the 1980s, the First Foursome featured Hope, Ford and O'Neill, along with a different pro each day, including the defending champion on the first day.

Hope and O'Neill may have been Ford's favorite amateur partners in the tournament, but Ford's all-time Hope highlight came in 1995. That year, on personal invitations from Hope, Ford was joined in a unique presidential threesome by sitting President Bill Clinton and former President George H.W. Bush.

While Clinton and Bush seemed to circle each other most of the day, with fans wondering just how the two recent political rivals could co-exist on a golf course,

Ford was able to sit back and relax, knowing he was friendly with both Clinton and Bush.

"That was probably the pinnacle of all tournaments, as far as political personalities were concerned," Ford said.

What seemed to endear Ford to the desert galleries as much as anything was that Ford was just as big a fan of the pros as the crowds were. In addition to opening the tournament in the foursome with the defending champion, Ford would always play a round during the week with Arnold Palmer, and when possible, with Jack Nicklaus.

While Palmer and Nicklaus were among his all-time favorite pro partners and both became friends of Ford through the years, Ford was never that comfortable

ABOVE: Former Speaker of the House, Tip O'Neill with President Gerald Ford, 1983. *Courtesy Bob Hope Classic archives*

RIGHT: A distinguished foursome of House Speaker Tip O'Neill, President Gerald Ford, Bob Hope and professional Tom Watson, 1982. *Courtesy Bob Hope Classic archives*

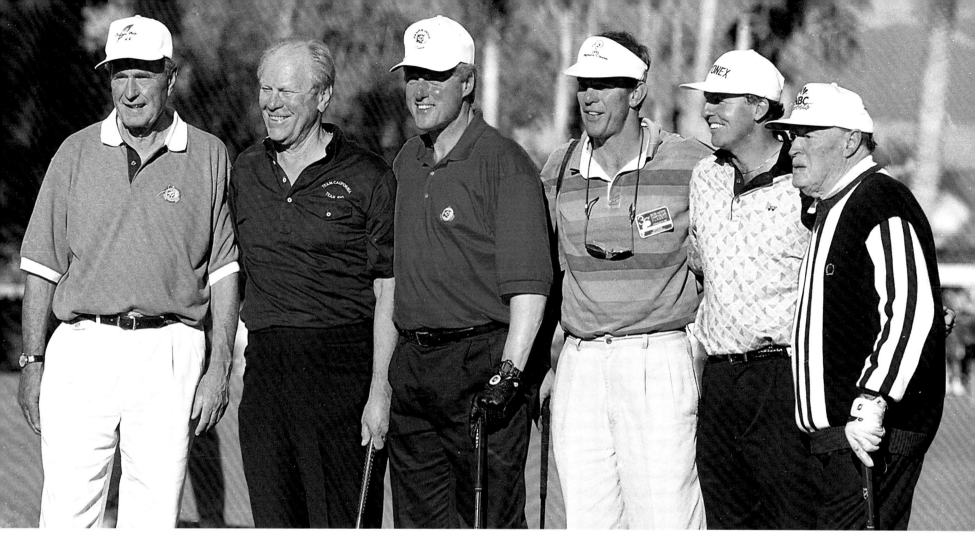

playing with the game's biggest stars.

"When I first started playing in pro-ams, particularly playing with Arnold and Jack, I was intimidated," he said. "But after several years of playing with them a number of times, I became less so. It's the crowd that they draw that intimidates me, really."

Ford's passion for the game ran deeper than just admiring the pros he was paired with or lending his name to pro-ams for charity. For years he hosted his own tournament in Vail, Colo., the Fords' summer home after he left office and a favorite spot for skiing until Ford's

knees became too painful.

By playing so much golf since leaving the presidency, Ford developed definite opinions about the game and the courses he had played.

"I don't have any close affinity with any golf course designer except Nicklaus and Palmer, who I play with," he said. "But I get a little upset with some of these golf course architects who make a golf course so tough for the amateur. That, I think, is unfair. More people play those courses who are amateurs than pros. I'm unhappy when I get out on a golf course that has a

ABOVE: Former presidents George H.W. Bush, Gerald Ford and Bill Clinton with Tom Baty, head course superintendent at Indian Wells Country Club; defending champion Scott Hoch, and Bob Hope in 1995.
Courtesy Desert Sun archives

great reputation for being a tough course. I like a course that is fun."

One reason Ford played with so many pros in the tournament was because he generally played all four pro-am rounds. That was unlike Hope, who by the late 1980s had taken to skipping the second or third rounds or sometimes both days, because of his busy schedule and his age.

In the years after O'Neill left the tournament, Hope officials tried to fill the final amateur berth with Ford and Hope with hot celebrities. That led to some inevitable eyebrow-raising when the pairings were announced. What was a dignified man like Gerald Ford doing in the same group as football bad boy Lawrence Taylor?

No matter what his pairing was, Ford also was happy to play because for at least two rounds he'd be playing with Hope.

"Bob Hope was the attraction for me and I think for most of the other political dignitaries," Ford said.

Ford's participation in the tournament was honored in 1997 when he was the third person inducted into the Indian Wells Classic Hall of Fame, behind Arnold Palmer and Hope.

But Ford's participation went beyond just showing up for his tee times or accepting an honor, as Ernie Dunlevie discovered during the 2000 tournament. That was the year Dunlevie, a five-time Classic president and a member at Indian Wells, was inducted into the Classic Hall of Fame.

It was an honor Dunlevie appreciated, being lumped in with Palmer, Hope, Ford and two-time Hope winner John Cook. But he was sure the induction ceremonies would lay a public relations egg.

"At first I said no, because it won't draw flies," Dunlevie said. "With all those big names, you stick me in there and nothing is going to happen. Well, I'll be damned if Ford didn't come. He just couldn't have been nicer."

Dunlevie had invited some of his business friends to the induction, and Ford even mingled with them.

"There they were with a drink in their hands, talking

to the former president of the United States. They just couldn't get over it," Dunlevie recalls. "These are very sophisticated businessmen, and they were just floored."

Eventually, Ford's age and his aching knees caught up with him and his golf game. In 1999, Ford didn't play a single round in the tournament, ending his long run as the tournament's elder statesman. Ford would still show up at the tournament at times, though, as a tribute to his close friend and golfing partner.

"I'm prejudiced, but I think Bob Hope is one of the outstanding citizens of the United States in the 20th century," Ford said.

"He was without a doubt, in my opinion, the most outstanding comedian across the years, not only in the United States but on a worldwide basis. I think Bob Hope will go down as a legend in the history of entertainment in this country." ∎

ABOVE: President Gerald Ford and Bob Hope in 1994. *Courtesy Bob Hope Classic archives*

OPPOSITE: The Classic's three great personalities, Arnold Palmer, Bob Hope and President Gerald Ford, share a moment on the first tee. The trio played together most years starting in 1977. *Courtesy Bob Hope Classic archives*

LEFT: NFL football player Lawrence Taylor, Bob Hope, President Gerald Ford and professional Raymond Floyd in 1991. *Courtesy Bob Hope Classic archives (bh92rsmis001)*

Keep'em Laughing

....

At its heart, the Bob Hope Chrysler Classic has always been a professional golf tournament first, a celebrity pro-am second. With a winner's list that includes names such as Palmer, Nicklaus, Casper, Miller, Kite, Couples, Duval and Mickelson, it is the brilliance of professional golfers that has taken center stage.

But without the tournament's five-decade association with the biggest and brightest names in entertainment and sports, the Hope could easily have blended in with so

many other PGA Tour events.

It is the celebrities that have distinguished it from Milwaukee, Fort Worth or Greensboro on the tour. And for nearly four of those decades, the sparkplug for the celebrity antics was the tournament host, Bob Hope. From comic ringleader to emcee to the man who could get almost anyone to agree to play the event, Hope was more than just a figurehead host.

"He was just another player like Desi (Arnaz) or any of the other celebrities," tournament board member Ernie Dunlevie said. "But having his name on it (starting in 1965), he became interested in the success of the tournament."

As one of the busiest entertainers in the world, Hope naturally had no time for monthly board meetings about the tournament. But as celebrity golf began to grow, with the addition of such names as Andy Williams, Glen Campbell, Dean Martin, Jackie Gleason, Danny Thomas and Sammy Davis Jr. to tournaments around the country, Hope remained engaged without inserting himself into the daily operations.

"Why I think our tournament was able to maintain a steady course is that Bob didn't get involved. The other celebrities were all making demands," Dunlevie said. "They had friends, these two guys want to play together and so on. Bob never did that."

Hope saw the celebrities in the tournament as a chance to attract fans with entertainment, not necessarily with good golf. That was perhaps the biggest difference between the Hope tournament in the desert and Bing Crosby's tournament on the Monterey Peninsula.

Crosby was very serious about his golf and wanted celebrities who could play the game. Hope wanted big names that could have fun on the course, even if it meant fudging a bit on the tournament's 18-handicap limit. And while Hope wasn't part of tournament operations, he was important to which celebrities played his event.

"Bob used to be very personally involved in picking the celebrities." said Ed Heorodt, who became Hope tournament director in 1981 after retiring from a long career as an advertising and marketing executive at Chrysler.

"I had a list of celebrities that we had the previous year, and I'd take that list up to Hope. We were supposed to have 18 at the time. I remember one year Hope was playing golf at Tamarisk … and I handed him this piece of paper, and I still remember he went down the list and put these big check marks next to the people he wanted, plus he added a few. I always used to go up to his house and go

ABOVE: Baseball Hall of Famer Ralph Kiner is seen in this undated photo from the Bob Hope Desert Classic. *Courtesy Desert Sun archives*

LEFT: Dancer and actor Ray Bolger, famous for his portrayal of the Scarecrow in *The Wizard of Oz,* was a crowd favorite in the 1960s and 1970s for his physical brand of comedy. *Courtesy Bob Hope Classic archives*

OPPOSITE LEFT: Danny Thomas gives a big smooch to Los Angeles Dodger pitching legend, Sandy Koufax, in 1967. *Courtesy Bob Hope Classic archives*

OPPOSITE RIGHT: Andy Williams and Lee Trevino in 1978. *Courtesy Bob Hope Classic archives*

over the list every year. Who do you want, Bob?"

As a member at Lakeside Country Club in the Los Angeles area, populated by a huge number of Hollywood stars, Hope had a cluster of golfing friends who he always wanted in the field.

Names like dancer and actor Ray Bolger and actor Buddy Rogers never needed to be approved, because Hope wanted them in the field every year.

In the late 1960s and early 1970s, with the Vietnam War raging and splitting the country apart, it was difficult to find legitimate American heroes who everyone admired and who wouldn't cause some disruptions or protests. The safest group seemed to be the astronauts of the Apollo program that took the United States to the moon.

Hope, ever the patriot, embraced the astronauts as part of his tournament.

"One thing that he always wanted was the astronauts," Heorodt said. "One year, one or two of them couldn't make it, and he was disappointed.

"One guy that always wanted to come back was Alan Shepard. (Bob) always wanted them on the list, and we tried our darnedest to get him there."

ABOVE: Flip Wilson, who hosted a variety show on NBC, joins Bob Hope and Sammy Davis, Jr. backstage at a Classic Ball, early 1980s. *Courtesy Bob Hope Classic archives*

LEFT: A colorful Glen Campbell was a fixture in the Hope tournament in the 1970s and 1980s. Campbell also hosted his own PGA Tour tournament in Los Angeles. *Courtesy Bob Hope Classic archives*

OPPOSITE LEFT: Clint Eastwood, who played in the golf tournament and the accompanying tennis tournament, in the 1970s. *Courtesy Bob Hope Classic archives*

OPPOSITE TOP RIGHT: World's wackiest caddie, Phyllis Diller equipped with a classic survival jacket in 1968. Bob Hope checks out the jacket as Gay Brewer looks on. *Courtesy Bob Hope Classic archives*

OPPOSITE BOTTOM RIGHT: Many NBC stars, including Dean Martin, played in the Hope tournament in the years it was broadcast on NBC. Martin was the host of a variety show on the network. *Courtesy Bob Hope Classic archives*

Shepard was the astronaut who made history repeatedly. He was the first American in space in 1961 and later walked on the moon as Apollo 14's commander. It was on that lunar excursion that Shepard attached the head of a 6-iron onto the handle of a rock collector, then dropped a couple of golf balls and hit the first intergalactic golf shots.

Hope would later take a certain amount of credit for Shepard's moon swings.

About a year before Shepard's walk on the moon, Hope toured NASA facilities and, as an honored guest, was rigged up in a harness that reproduced the near-

ABOVE: Astronaut Alan Shepard, the first American in space who later walked on the moon, played in three Hopes in the 1970s, four times in the 1980s and three times in the 1990s. *Courtesy Bob Hope Classic archives*

RIGHT: Astronaut Gene Cernan played in five Hope Tournaments from 1972-1978. Here, he discusses golf clubs with actor Robert Stack. *Courtesy Bob Hope Classic archives*

weightlessness astronauts feel on the moon. Hope said he was so surprised by the effect of the harness that he used his ever-present golf club to help balance himself.

As the story goes, Shepard, in the room at the time, saw Hope use the club and was inspired to pull off the lunar shots.

The two swings on the moon made Shepard a superstar among golfers and a natural for the Hope. Trying to make Shepard feel as comfortable at Bermuda Dunes in the 1972 tournament as he did on the moon, Hope's tournament convinced NASA to allow Shepard and Hope to roam around the golf course in the actual cart used as a training vehicle for astronauts for the lunar rover, the electric car used for exploring the moon's surface.

While the celebrities provided the show, Hope was always searching for new ways to inject entertainment into the event. One year, shortly after he began lending his name to the tournament, Hope toured Japan and saw something he wanted to bring back to the desert: Women dressed in full geisha regalia as caddies.

Upon his return, Hope immediately told Classic officials it would be a terrific idea to bring a handful of the geisha girls over to caddie for some of the celebrities.

Arrangements were made and six women were brought to the 1968 tournament. Hope joked that the only rule was that celebrities had to give the geishas back at the end of each round. No souvenirs, he said. Hope would later credit Ernie Dunlevie of the tournament board with the idea, but Dunlevie insists the gag was pure Hope.

The tournament board was willing to listen to Hope on issues about celebrities and golf because he knew almost everyone in Hollywood in the 1960s through the 1980s. There never was a doubt about his passion for the sport, said Dwayne Netland. He co-wrote Hope's book, "Bob Hope's Confessions of a Hooker: My Lifelong Love Affair with Golf," and saw that love firsthand while assisting Hope with the book.

"He wanted to play every day," Netland said. "One time in St. Louis, this is September of 1983, the first year we were working on the book, we were in the Chase Hotel. He kept looking outside. I said, 'Bob, it must be 100 degrees out there and it's humid as hell.' He said, 'Let's go hit some balls.'

"So, he heads down to this crummy little driving range, with Dolores coming along. Here are all these locals popping their beer cans, and here comes Bob Hope, whacking away at a bucket of balls."

Just how good of a player was Hope in his days as tournament chairman? Everyone agrees that Hope could be a good player, but that his handicap and his game began to slip as the years caught up with him.

"I guess his best game was around a 6 to an 8 handicap," former tournament director Bill Yancey said. "I don't know how he could ever play that well as poor a putter as he was. Because he was the world's worst putter. He would take the most lovely practice swing and then everything would stop before he got to the ball."

Hope and the directors of his tournament always understood that for many of the celebrities, the tournament was a chance to get on television – if they were in the so-called "A" field that was the focus of Saturday's broadcast. In later years, the tournament would make sure that all the celebrities were in the A field, along

with the most popular professionals.

The tournament hummed along in the 1960s and 1970s with big-name tournament winners and a solid group of celebrities. In many cases, the stars that played in Hope's event had tournaments of their own, and Hope would try to reciprocate and play in theirs when his busy schedule would allow.

That might mean a trip to San Diego for Andy Williams' tournament, or to Miami for Jackie Gleason's tournament, and certainly an appearance in Crosby's Clambake.

But the 1980s saw significant changes in the Hope.

ABOVE: Jackie Gleason and Hope on stage at during the 1980 Classic Ball. *Courtesy Bob Hope Classic archives*

RIGHT: Jackie Gleason admires the pants worn by Bob Hope during the 1978 Classic. *Courtesy Bob Hope Classic archives*

First, celebrity golf tournaments were under pressure as corporate sponsorships began to grow.

By 1985, for example, more than seven years after he died, Bing Crosby's name was taken off the Monterey Peninsula by his widow, who said the tournament had lost its Clambake feel as AT&T became the event's corporate sponsor.

Williams left the San Diego tournament after 1988 after having shared the title with a car manufacturer, a furniture store and a financial company. Five years earlier, Glen Campbell's name was gone from Los Angeles,

ABOVE: Huey Lewis signs autographs for fans during the 2009 Classic at Silver Rock Resort. *Courtesy Desert Sun archives*

TOP RIGHT: 1971 Contestant button belonging to Willie Mays. *Courtesy Bob Hope Classic archives*

BOTTOM RIGHT: Two-time Hope Winner John Mahaffey prepares to tee off with his amateur threesome, baseball great Willie Mays, board member Vic Lobue and Lou McAnich. Lobue was co-owner of Indian Wells Country Club and was the only amateur to win the Hope Amateur tournament three times. *Courtesy Bob Hope Classic archives*

OPPOSITE TOP LEFT: June MacMurray, actor Fred MacMurray, Arnold Palmer and Hurbert Green in 1974. *Courtesy Bob Hope Classic archives*

OPPOSITE MIDDLE LEFT: Radio personality Rick Dees hams it up with a young fans during one of his numerous starts in the 1990s. *Courtesy Bob Hope Classic archives*

OPPOSITE BOTTOM LEFT: Actor Leslie Nielsen poses with 1994 Classic Girls Michelle Watters, Sandra Howard and Heather Applin. *Courtesy Bob Hope Classic archives*

OPPOSITE RIGHT: Payne Stewart with William Devane in 1996. *Courtesy Desert Sun archives*

eventually replaced by Nissan.

In fact, by 1990, Hope was the only celebrity who was hosting a PGA Tour event. And while there was now corporate sponsorship for Hope's tournament, too, it was in the form of an old Hope and tournament friend, Chrysler.

In 1985, the word "Desert" was replaced by "Chrysler" in the title of the tournament, but Chrysler had been part of the tournament since Hope officially joined the event in 1965.

"In the early days, they bought the whole show," Dunlevie said. "Then, as the price went up, they shared with other sponsors. When they became title sponsor, they actually put some money into the tournament."

Another change focused on the celebrities playing

in the event. Stars such as Kirk Douglas, Desi Arnaz and Dean Martin from the 1960s and 1970s weren't playing in the event as much. They were replaced by more professional athletes, such big names as Marcus Allen, Michael Jordan, Lawrence Taylor and Mark McGwire.

As Hope passed his 80th birthday in 1983, his traditional ties to Hollywood were starting to soften. It was hard for him to keep up with the hottest names in the next generation of stars.

A perfect example: Grammy Award-winning singer Huey Lewis. He was the lead singer for the platinum-selling band, Huey Lewis and the News, who scorched the charts with a string of hits in the mid- to late-80s. The group also was huge with Bay Area sports fans, often singing the national anthem at football or baseball games.

Lewis seemed a natural to be added to the field – if Hope only had known who Lewis was.

"I put (Lewis') name down and took it to Hope. He looked down and saw 'Huey Lewis' and he said, 'Who's that?' " Heorodt said. "That was it. He was out."

ABOVE: The clubhouse and view behind the 18th green at the Eldorado County Club, 1980s.
Courtesy Bob Hope Classic archives

RIGHT: Thirteenth hole at the PGA West Stadium Course. *Courtesy Bob Hope Classic archives*

FAR RIGHT: The 18th hole at La Quinta Country Club, circa 1970. The course was dropped into a three-year rotation with Eldorado and Tamarisk in 1987
Courtesy Bob Hope Classic archives

OPPOSITE: Tamarisk Country Club. Hole 2 of the 2002 Bob Hope Chrysler Classic. *Courtesy Bob Hope Classic archives*

As the 1980s closed, one final change emerged: the Hope Tournament courses themselves.

The older Hope courses built in the 1950s were starting to show their age. The pros, improving with better equipment and new technology, were assaulting the older, shorter courses with lower scores annually. And as the older private country clubs built more and more on open land once used by the tournament, it was getting tougher to hold the event at the original venues.

For the 1987 tournament, La Quinta Country Club, a permanent course in the event since 1964, dropped into a three-year rotation with Eldorado and Tamarisk. That opened the door for perhaps the most controversial golf course in the country to join the Hope, the TPC Stadium Course at PGA West.

Course designer Pete Dye had been given marching orders from developers Ernie Vossler and Joe Walser to build "the toughest damn golf course in the world." Dye obliged with a vengeance.

The Stadium Course was everything the other Hope courses weren't. While the older courses were all built in the 1950s, the Stadium Course was a tribute to man's new

ability to move dirt.

The other Hope courses were generally flat or incorporated the natural desert dunes. Dye's design for the Stadium Course completely reshaped the desert floor of La Quinta.

Long, deep bunkers, including a 19-foot-deep bunker at the green, stretched nearly the length of the 16th hole. A sand moat surrounded the 12th green. The par-3 sixth hole could stretch to 255 yards, all over water. The 11th hole was 611 yards, and the par-5 featured water against the left side of the green.

While other Hope courses were criticized for being too easy and too short, the Stadium Course quickly established a reputation as a terrifying and torturous track.

No one would shoot 62 on this course, and no one could complain about the tournament being too easy anymore.

In fact, just the opposite happened. While the Stadium Course had been used in the 1986 Skins Game, a match-play format with just four players, the 1987 Hope was the first chance for the rest of the tour to see the course – and many players didn't like what they saw.

"You want to put some dynamite to it," Ken Green said after a 4-over 76 at the course. "I hit a shot five feet from the hole and it ends up 50 feet away, and I think that's out of hand."

"I've had enough of this for one day," former Hope winner Craig Stadler said after a 75. "Miss a fairway out here and you're dead. The golf course doesn't seem to

---

TOP SERIES: Corey Pavin reacts to sinking a 20-foot putt on the final hole to win the 1987 Hope. This tournament was the only time the event was played on the TPC Stadium Course at PGA West. *Courtesy Bob Hope Classic archives*

LEFT: Pavin celebrates his 1987 victory in the Hope tournament. His final round, 67, was the best round of the week at the TPC Stadium Course.
Courtesy Bob Hope Classic archives

LEFT: Jack Lemmon smokes a cigarette while taking a back swing in the 1980s. *Courtesy Desert Sun archives*

BOTTOM LEFT: Orel Hershiser, ace pitcher for the Los Angeles Dodgers, signs an autograph during the 1990 Classic. Baseball players were popular additions to the pro- am in the 1980s and 1990s. *Courtesy Desert Sun archives*

BOTTOM MIDDLE: Football star Emmitt Smith and radio commentator Rush Limbaugh meet with President Gerald Ford before teeing off in the 2001 Classic at the Arnold Palmer Course at PGA West. *Courtesy Bob Hope Classic archives*

BELOW: Singer Frankie Avalon follows his shot in the 1996 Classic. *Courtesy Desert Sun archives*

give you a break. If you don't hit two perfect shots, you're looking at a bogey."

Two-time U.S. Open champion Curtis Strange simply referred to the course as "difficult," later relaying his mother's advice: If you can't say anything nice, don't say anything at all.

In defense of the course, horrible weather hit the desert the first and third days of the event. The rain and cold winds made the difficult course even tougher. Additionally, the course had only been open about a year, and the greens were still a bit immature.

Still, for a tournament where 20 under was generally only good enough for a top-10 finish, Corey Pavin managed a final-round 67 at the Stadium Course for a winning score of 17 under. The higher scores seemed a direct result of the change in courses.

Compounding the problem was the course rotation for the year, which had the golfers playing the Stadium Course the day after playing the easiest course in the tournament, Indian Wells Country Club. Scores plummeted significantly.

It did not go unnoticed by Hope. He quipped, "The back tees are in Hemet."

For his part, Dye professed a certain glee that the

OPPOSITE LEFT: Yogi Berra reacts to missing a close putt after he made a more difficult shot to the green during the 2008 Classic. *Courtesy Desert Sun archives*

OPPOSITE RIGHT: NFL stars Marcus Allen, left, and Sterling Sharpe joke around after putting at Tamarisk Country Club in 2005. *Courtesy Desert Sun archives*

BOTTOM LEFT: President Gerald Ford with NFL star Jerry Rice, 1998. *Courtesy Bob Hope Classic archives*

BOTTOM RIGHT: Glenn Frey reacts to his drive from the 10th tee at Indian Wells Country Club during the first day of the 2002 Bob Hope Chrysler Classic. *Courtesy Desert Sun archives*

players were struggling with his course, even with the most modern of clubs and golf balls that Dye thought had made other courses obsolete.

Still, he was a bit confused at the ferocity of the attacks on his course.

Standing in the back of the press room one day during the event, Dye shook his head and told a reporter, "Any golfer will tell you the Mountain Course (at nearby La Quinta Hotel) is a tougher course."

Within a week, the rumor sprung up that a petition was being circulated among the pros at the Los Angeles Open asking the tour to drop the Stadium Course from the Hope.

In reality, Heorodt said, the decision was already made.

"Walter Probst was president that year. You know what it's like to finish a golf tournament. You've met all your deadlines and Monday you're pooped," Heorodt said.

"Well, Walter called a meeting for 8 a.m. Monday morning at the Classic office. Some of the players had gotten to him and never wanted to play that golf course again. So Monday morning at 8 a.m., with (PGA Commissioner) Deane Beman in attendance, we made a decision to never play that golf course again."

Change was indeed coming to the Bob Hope Chrysler Classic as the 1980s ended. But even bigger challenges were on the horizon. ■

ABOVE: Actors Samuel L. Jackson and Joe Pesci share a conversation on the 10th tee at Indian Wells Country Club during the first day of the 2002 Bob Hope Chrysler Classic. *Courtesy Desert Sun archives*

RIGHT: President Gerald Ford with actor Leslie Nielsen, 1997. *Courtesy Bob Hope Classic archives*

FAR RIGHT: Glen Campbell tries to coax his putt with a little body language. Campbell played in the tournament 28 years. *Courtesy Bob Hope Classic archives*

Hail to the Chiefs

When the Bob Hope Chrysler Classic board of directors called a last-minute news conference on Feb. 7, 1995, reporters assumed they knew the story.

It was anticipated that George H.W. Bush, the nation's 41st president and the grandson of a United States Golf Association president, would be joining another former Republican president, Gerald Ford, in the tournament's famous First Foursome. They would team with Hope and defending champion Scott Hoch.

What the Hope board had up its sleeve that day, though, was perhaps the best-kept secret in tournament history, if not PGA Tour history. Tournament president John Foster announced that a third commander-in-chief, then-President Bill Clinton, would be joining the group for a day to form the tournament's first "fivesome."

"I think it's a credit to Bob Hope, who has meant so much to golf and to America and, quite frankly, to the presidency," Foster told stunned reporters.

ABOVE: The official first tee portrait in 1995 features President George H.W. Bush, professional and defending champion Scott Hoch, PGA Commissioner Tim Finchem, President Bill Clinton, Bob Hope and President Gerald Ford. *Courtesy Bob Hope Classic archives*

Hope, at the age of 91, helped pull off a coup in the combined arenas of golf, show business and politics. He had personally invited Clinton and Bush to play in the tournament in letters delivered just before Christmas. He then followed up with telephone calls.

"Bob called Clinton," Dolores Hope said. "And he was a nice man. … He couldn't have been nicer."

Hope's name and reputation as an American and golfing icon had brought together two of the most bitter rivals in recent political history.

It was hard to envision Bush agreeing to play a friendly 18 holes with the former Arkansas governor who had defeated him in the 1992 election and described him as being out-of-touch with the common man.

But, the former World War II fighter pilot who succeeded Ronald Reagan did exactly that.

It was equally surprising that a sitting Democratic president would want to venture to the Coachella Valley, a Republican stronghold that was the post-White House home of popular Republican Gerald Ford.

But this visit was different.

No one questioned that Bush would get the bigger ovations and would draw more fans to the tournament than Clinton. But a kind of Clinton-mania swept through the Palm Springs area that week. Most valley golf fans figured that if you couldn't respect the highly controversial Clinton as president, one had to respect his office and his willingness to put his much-discussed golf game on display.

The Clinton-Bush tandem made history on several levels. Clinton became the first president to play in a PGA Tour event while still in office. Bush had played in the pro-am of the 1990 Doug Sanders Celebrity Classic, an official Senior PGA Tour event in the Houston suburb of Kingwood. But that was just the pro-am before the tournament.

At the Hope, Clinton and Bush would be playing alongside a PGA Tour player – in this case, defending champion Hoch – whose score for the day would count in the official tournament.

The Clinton-Bush pairing was just the latest in a long line of political visits to the Classic. Through golf and his work entertaining American troops overseas, Hope was closer to the nation's highest seat of power than perhaps any other civilian in history.

His status as an American legend and host of a golf tournament made it easy for him to call on some of his Washington buddies to make the trip to Palm Springs to occasionally play in the Desert Classic.

Who could refuse?

Hope's tournament offered face time on national TV for something non-partisan. A vice president or congressman could even look human, wearing slacks and a sweater instead of a gray suit. They could joke with athletes and actors, while still serving as good-natured targets to Hope's jabs.

And Hope never discriminated against either political party. Everyone was fair game to be skewered.

When talking about Ronald Reagan, for instance, Hope was more likely to mock Reagan's age or his affinity for horses and jelly beans than to joke about the Iran-Contra scandal ("He broke 100 the other day, which isn't bad for a man on horseback," Hope said.)

Barbs were made about John F. Kennedy's matinee good looks, not the Cuban Missile Crisis.

It was political humor for mass consumption and it worked for seven decades.

News of the Clinton-Bush appearance triggered a frenzy among fans. Officials were inundated with calls for tickets and information.

It was later learned that Bush had eagerly agreed to play in the tournament, but he apparently was surprised to learn tournament officials planned to put him in the same group with Clinton. It fell to board member Ernie Dunlevie to deliver the news through a close friend of Bush's, Arnold Palmer.

It was a memorable phone call.

"He said, 'Ernie, I'm here with President Bush and he wants to know if it's true who he is supposed to play with.'" Dunlevie said.

"Now, this is just one week before the tournament. I said, 'Yes, Arnold, I'm afraid it's true.' … (Arnold) turned to George Bush and said, 'I just got it from the horse's mouth.'"

Dunlevie was afraid Bush might renege on the appearance. But while Bush might have felt blindsided by the pairing, he carried through with his commitment.

"I think it was well known there was some lack of a

ABOVE: President Bush and two-time Hope winner Corey Pavin share some lockerroom banter.
Courtesy Bob Hope Classic archives

OPPOSITE: Three presidents enjoy a moment with Classic fixture Glen Campbell. *Courtesy Bob Hope Classic archives*

deep friendship between Bush and Clinton," said Gerald Ford, the third president in the group.

"I guess it went back to the campaign. But they were more than anxious to appear to be friends just in deference to Bob Hope. Bob really put the pressure on them, all three of us, really, to come. We did it because of our loyalty and friendship to Bob."

Ironically, 10 years later, Bush and Clinton would form a friendship when they were asked by President George W. Bush to spearhead private fundraising efforts for tsunami victims in Asia. But in 1995, the relationship was cool at best.

Whether the tournament had pulled a fast one on Bush or Bush's own people simply failed in communicating with their boss, the Bob Hope Chrysler Classic had pulled off a coup unrivaled by any tournament on tour.

The Hope was now on the network evening news and the front page of more than just the local paper. And with the official announcement eight days before the round, the Classic would be the focus of national attention for a full week.

It was the kind of publicity an old vaudevillian like Hope could revel in for years.

Getting Clinton and Bush to play together was one thing. Pulling off the logistics was another thing entirely.

Six days before Clinton and Bush teed off, a C-141 Starlifter military transport plane arrived at the Palm Springs airport. On board was Clinton's advance team, including a fleet of security specialists faced with the unique task of protecting a president who had agreed to walk around a country club for five hours or more in front of 20,000 or more fans.

"We had a week prior to the event to spend some time with these guys," said Mark Neneman, general manager of Indian Wells Country Club. "There were probably six people or so who came out with their advance team, one security guy, one Secret Service guy, some guy from their

press corps, a communications guy.

"They arrived that weekend and basically for the next week, almost 10, 11 hours a day, that's all I did, spend time with them. And we went through everything you could imagine."

In the days leading up to the historic round, Indian Wells staff members were subject to full background and security checks. Bomb-sniffing dogs checked out the clubhouse and other areas of the country club. Chemicals and fertilizers considered potentially dangerous were removed even from outer maintenance buildings.

Another major concern was the rugged mountains that run along the south side of the course.

"They had people in camouflage on the mountains," Neneman said. "There were probably four guys in the mountains, plus a helicopter. You never saw it. It was a perimeter deal."

Wherever the president goes, the White House press corps is never far behind. That meant the tournament had to provide a second media tent at Indian Wells to accommodate the 150 or so members of Clinton's press entourage. Television and radio stations from Los Angeles and San Diego clamored for credentials. Newspapers and magazines that traditionally asked for one credential sought four or five.

Clinton and his party arrived in the desert the night before the tournament after the president delivered a Valentine's Day speech in San Bernardino, about a one-hour drive from Indian Wells. Clinton made the trip by presidential helicopter to nearby Bermuda Dunes Airport, then traveled in a motorcade to the Hyatt Grand Champions Resort, which is across the street from Indian Wells Country Club.

Bush was staying at the private estate of Walter Annenberg, an old friend, former ambassador to England and publishing magnate. His private desert estate, Sunnylands, at Frank Sinatra and Bob Hope drives in Rancho Mirage, includes an ultra-private, by-invitation-only nine-hole golf course. The estate is about a long par-

ABOVE: President Clinton eyes an approach shot early in the round. *Courtesy Bob Hope Classic archives*

RIGHT: President Bill Clinton enjoys a relaxed moment during the round. *Courtesy Bob Hope Classic archives*

OPPOSITE: President Gerald Ford watches his shot as President George Bush looks on.
Courtesy Bob Hope Classic archives

5 from the Hope tournament office.

Sunnylands had hosted Bush before, as well as his predecessor, Ronald Reagan.

Fans entering Indian Wells Country Club that day were greeted by unprecedented security, including Secret Service agents and metal detectors.

The crowds were huge for a tournament played in one of the smallest markets on the PGA Tour. Extra stands were erected, but the gallery spilled over from the 10th hole, where the fivesome would begin their day, toward the nearby 14th and 16th greens on the tight back nine of Indian Wells.

At least 20,000 were on the course, far more than the 12,000 Neneman said he would expect for a normal celebrity day of the tournament. And they all wanted to watch one group.

Almost from the start, the day's schedule was out of whack. Clinton was expected to arrive last among the three presidents after a morning jog. But he was so excited by the round that he came to the course early and was the first of the fivesome to arrive. He walked into the clubhouse, where he ran into an unsuspecting Ernie Dunlevie.

"All of a sudden, this door bursts open, and I was so shocked I wasn't fully aware of who it was," Dunlevie said. "But he walks right over to me and says, 'Hi, I'm Bill Clinton.' I said, 'Hi, I'm Ernie Dunlevie.' He said, 'Nice to meet you.' It was like he was still running for office. Then at least 20 Secret Service guys followed him into the locker room."

For Clinton, who was not as avid a player as the other two presidents, one concern for the day was not committing a dumb mistake on the course.

"Clinton was very nervous about all the proper etiquette and what he needed to do when he was out on the golf course," Neneman said. "I mean he was very concerned that he would do something wrong as a player in front of everybody."

Just before 9 a.m., about an hour before he was

scheduled to tee off, Clinton walked on to the driving range wearing a red golf shirt with a Hope logo and an Indian Wells cap, both provided by the club.

The president received polite applause from fans who were packed onto one of the smallest driving ranges in the desert. A few minutes later, the crowd erupted for Bush's appearance. He wore a blue Classic shirt and stayed surrounded by his own entourage, away from Clinton's group. Ford and Hope arrived about 15 minutes after that to their typical huge applause.

"I don't think we even thought about that, how popular they were one against the other," Dunlevie said. "I guess we assumed that the president, regardless of who he was, would get respect and applause. I don't think it occurred to us that Bush would get more or Hope would get more."

The group gathered for photos. Bush and Clinton seemed to keep their distance from one another, while Ford seemed to be having the most fun of the group.

"I was relaxed. I had played in the tournament so many times, it wasn't unique," Ford said. "I didn't have any tension between me and Clinton or me and Bush. It was a fun day as far as I was concerned."

The magnitude of the pairing was reflected in a simple fact: The legendary Palmer, playing in the group ahead of the fivesome, was hardly noticed on this day.

The receptions at the driving range were repeated when the group was introduced on the tee. Bush drew huge applause; Clinton drew appreciative acknowledgment.

The day's first awkward moment came on the 10th tee, where the fivesome would begin their round. Which of the presidents would hit first? Neneman said it was less a question of protocol than a matter of nerves.

"The first three or four holes were probably lined from tee to green with people 10, 15, 20 people deep," he said. "I felt sorry for them. I wouldn't have wanted to be up on that first tee.

"They were trying to decide who was going to have

ABOVE: President Bill Clinton and Bob Hope watch Hope's putt. *Courtesy Bob Hope Classic archives*

RIGHT: President George Bush contemplates his next shot during the round. *Courtesy Bob Hope Classic archives*

OPPOSITE TOP: Host Bob Hope shows appreciation for the activites of the day. *Courtesy Bob Hope Classic archives*

OPPOSITE BOTTOM: President Gerald Ford and President Bill Clinton share a hug during the round.
Courtesy Bob Hope Classic archives

honors, and nobody wanted to go first. And you saw a little uneasiness between the three of them at the time, very nervous and nobody wanted to get up there and hit the ball."

Eventually, the presidents teed off in the order of their assigned handicaps for the day; Clinton first, Bush second and Ford last.

With so many people lining the fairways to see golfers of questionable talent, it seemed inevitable that some fan was going to get hit. Bush and Ford took care of that quickly. Both hooked drives into the crowd off the 10th tee, with Ford's shot drawing some blood from the hand of a fan.

Bush's second shot on the par-4 10th hole headed toward the trees to the left of the fairway, glanced off a branch and the hit the nose of 71-year-old Norma Earley. The impact sent the woman to the ground and broke her sunglasses, leaving a cut from her nose to above her eyebrow.

Bush came over to the woman, whose husband was working as a volunteer at the tournament. After shaking Earley's hand and being assured she would be fine, Bush went back and continued the round. The cut was a nasty one, however, and Earley received 10 stitches at Eisenhower Medical Center.

Earley, a Republican and a Bush fan, said she wasn't switching parties over the incident.

The group was followed by a fleet of cameramen, deputies and Secret Service agents in carts. On one of them, unknown to the gallery, was the so-called "football," the case that gives the president control of the nation's nuclear weapons arsenal.

"It was pretty wild, because that golf cart broke down on the 15th hole, and we had to bring a new golf cart out for that," Neneman recalled. "That was a pretty big deal. That was a moment for a lot of tension on their part."

The round went pretty much as expected. Clinton, the youngest of the trio of presidents, had the better swing but seemed to have the most rust on his game. Bush,

using a broomstick putter, didn't play well but made the only birdie among the presidents, a 2 on the par-3 15th. Ford struggled with his game most of the day but hovered just over bogey golf with a few exceptions.

Hope, 91 at the time, would tee off occasionally, or might drop a ball in a fairway and hit to the green, then putt out. But he played all 18 holes.

"About the eighth hole, I said, 'Mr. Hope, we've got some lunch set up in the lockerroom. We can bring you in there and you can stop, then go out and rejoin these guys on the last few holes and play in,' " Neneman said.

"And he said, 'If the presidents are playing, I'm playing, and I'm going on.' And he did it. From what I know, that's probably one of the last times he played 18 holes of golf in a single period of time."

At the end of the day, Bush, playing to the tournament maximum of an 18 handicap, had gained a measure of

revenge against Clinton. He managed a 92, including the one birdie. Clinton, listed as an 11 but playing like a man who might have neglected his game since being elected, was credited with a 94. Like Bush, though, the actual score was no doubt a few shots higher.

Ford polished off a 102 with a par on the final hole.

In what has to go down as one of the great rounds in PGA Tour history, Hoch shot a bogey-free 70. True, that left him seven shots behind first-round leader Kenny Perry, who had played miles away in total obscurity at Indian Ridge Country Club that day. But under the circumstances, Hoch's round of 16 pars and two birdies deserved special merit.

"You always want to play well as the defending champion and especially with all the President's men here," Hoch told reporters after the round. "I wouldn't have traded today for anything."

After the round, the club hosted some small ceremonies for the presidents. It gave them a chance to relax, meet with the celebrities and for Bush to lodge his one complaint.

Bush is a notoriously fast player, known for playing 18 holes in under two hours on some occasions. The Classic round that day had stretched over five hours. Bush revealed just how tough the first hole was on the nerves of the presidents.

"He said, 'It was a great time, but I tell you, it was probably one of the worst times when we stood up on that first hole,' " Neneman said. "He said he was in some European country, maybe the Vatican, where he had to stand up in front to 200,000 or 300,000 people, to give a speech, which wasn't a problem for him.

"But he said, 'When I stood up on that tee today, in front of all those people and looked down that fairway, it was one of the biggest fears I've ever had.' " Dunlevie said.

Clinton's day of golf wasn't over just yet. As the ceremonies ended, Hoch approached Clinton to give the president a driver.

"He was so excited, he turned to me and said, 'Mark,

ABOVE: The crowd shows appreciation for a long putt by President Bush. *Courtesy Bob Hope Classic archives*

LEFT: President Clinton becomes familiar with the hazards of the mountain that borders Indian Wells Country Club. *Courtesy Bob Hope Classic archives*

OPPOSITE: President Clinton extricates himself from one of Indian Wells bunkers. *Courtesy Bob Hope Classic archives*

OPPOSITE: Board member John Foster talks with President Clinton in the Indian Wells clubhouse after the historic round. *Courtesy Bob Hope Classic archives*

BELOW: Scorecard from the first round of the 1995 Bob Hope Classic. Somehow professional Scott Hoch managed to shoot a two under 70. *Courtesy Bob Hope Classic archives*

can we go out on the driving range and hit some balls?'" Neneman said. "I said, whatever you want. So here we go out the back door of the locker room with probably 30-odd people, half of them being Secret Service. We go out on the range, and there are a couple of pros out there, if I remember right, Mark O'Meara was out there hitting balls.

"They are cleaning the place up and here comes this entourage. And he spends probably the next 20 or 25 minutes hitting balls. The sun is going down and the whole driving range is in shadows and he says, 'This is just a beautiful place, I love this, I'd like to come back out here.'"

By 5:30 p.m., Clinton was climbing aboard Air Force One, professing glee to reporters that he hadn't hurt anyone.

Moments later his 747 was in the air and the most historic round of bipartisan golf had become another chapter in the rich history of Bob Hope's golf tournament.

"I think that is one of the great days of history, and in golf history," Dolores Hope said. "They will never top that." ◾

PRO # 27   TEAM # 27   TEE 10   TIME 10:04

INDIAN WELLS COUNTRY CLUB   WEDNESDAY February 15, 1995

HOLES		1	2	3	4	5	6	7	8	9	OUT	10	11	12	13	14	15	16	17	18	IN	TOTAL
Pro: SCOTT HOCH		4	4	4	3	4	3	4	5	4	35	4	3	4	3	5	3	4	4	5	35	70
Par		4	4	4	3	5	3	4	5	4	36	4	4	4	3	5	3	4	4	5	36	72
Championship Yardage		388	355	382	162	517	140	338	515	398	3195	446	398	343	197	483	163	354	398	501	3283	6478
Amateur Team	Hcp.	3	13	1	15	7	17	11	9	5		2	6	14	10	16	18	8	4	12		
BILL CLINTON	11	6	4	6	3	6	4	5	7	5	46	7	7	5	4	5	6	4	5	5	48	94
GEORGE BUSH	18	4	6	7	4	8	4	5	5	4	47	7	5	5	4	5	2	6	5	6	45	92
HOPE / FORD	18	4	7	5	4	7	4	6	7	4	48	7	8	7	4	5	4	6	6	7	54	102
Best Ball																						

PROFESSIONAL'S SIGNATURE *Scott Hoch* ✓   3

TEAM CAPTAIN'S SIGNATURE *Mark Russell* / DATE

A new frontier: Washington, Hollywood and the desert

T he Clinton-Bush round in 1995 came 25 years after Bob Hope's tournament gained acclaim for successfully blending the worlds of golf, celebrity and politics.

Dwight Eisenhower had attended the first few tournaments and was on hand those years for the presentation of the trophy that bore his name, but the former World War II hero and president never played in the event.

In 1970, though, the Classic hosted the man who was the proverbial one heartbeat from becoming the most powerful man in the world, Vice President Spiro Agnew.

During the late 1960s and early 1970s, Agnew became a lightning rod for some of the nation's biggest foreign and domestic upheavals. That made him a popular target for students protesting America's involvement in the Vietnam War.

His participation in the 1970 Hope was limited to a single round on the fourth day of the tournament, but that round became the stuff of legend. Agnew's playing partners for the round were Hope, movie dancer-turned-U.S. Senator George Murphy of California and pro Doug Sanders, one of the tour's colorful and fun-loving characters.

On the first hole at La Quinta Country Club, after Sanders had hit from the professional tees, Agnew rifled a drive that hooked so wildly it cleared the heads of the gallery in the left rough.

"He was really hopeless. He was worse than Ford ever was," Classic director Ernie Dunlevie said of Agnew. "He was all over the place."

Sanders, who had played in enough pro-ams to know better, then made a cardinal error: He lost track of his

OPPOSITE: Trophy presentation in 1969. Dolores Hope, Billy Casper, Vice President Spiro Agnew, and Classic Queen Barbara Anderson, who would later star as a secretary on the televisions show Ironside. Bob Hope was not at the tournament in 1969 because he was doing USO shows for the troops. *Courtesy Bob Hope Classic archives*

LEFT: Typical star-studded moment from Classic history features, from left, actor Chuck Connors, Bob Hope, baseball great Willie Mays, NBC broadcaster Cary Middlecoff, Vice President Spiro Agnew, singer Glen Campbell and professional Doug Sanders, 1971.
Courtesy Bob Hope Classic archives

BELOW: Bruce Devlin displays his check for winning the 1970 Classic as Bob Hope and Vice President Spiro Agnew look on during the trophy presentation ceremony.
Courtesy Bob Hope Classic archives

playing partners.

Agnew wandered into the rough only to find his ball on a cart path. But Agnew didn't move the ball as he could have under the rules. Instead, he hit a 3-wood, and the face of the club opened up and slammed the ball almost directly to the right. That's where Sanders was standing, distracted by one of the Classic queens.

Before Sanders had a chance to react to the warning yells of the fans, the ball made a beeline for the pro and hit him squarely in the head.

"My hand was full of blood, and they had to hold me up. I staggered, but I never really went down," Sanders said.

If Agnew had felt badly about hitting Sanders, Hope and tournament officials were delighted to be given a little comic fodder. Agnew, Hope joked, had succeeded in turning golf into a contact sport.

Agnew was again invited to the tournament in 1971 and accepted another one-day visit for the fourth round. For Saturday's round at Bermuda Dunes Country Club, the Classic again arranged for Agnew and Hope to be paired with Sanders. Agnew, unfortunately, obliged the crowd, hitting not one but two people with his drive and a mulligan.

When Agnew accepted another invitation to play in 1972, Hope and his gag writers were waiting for him. Again, Sanders was the pro, with Hope and Frank Sinatra rounding out the foursome at Indian Wells Country Club.

By this time, Agnew was famous for his battles with student protesters, so Hope provided a few mock protesters on the first tee. The picket signs read, "He only hits the ones he loves," and, "Try the fairway, you'll like it."

This time, Agnew – who never objected to Hope's ribbing – didn't hit anyone in his group or in the gallery.

What reporters didn't know and never reported was that Agnew, Sinatra and Sanders enjoyed the day more than anyone could have known. Paul Jenkins, a board member of the Hope, had been assigned the task of driving around a beverage cart – strictly non-alcoholic – for the group.

That wasn't enough for this group, though.

"I called someone over and said, 'Go get a bottle of

vodka,'" Jenkins said. "He came back with the bottle wrapped up in a towel. It looked like he was carrying the Baby Jesus."

The thermos was filled with vodka, flavored with a splash of orange juice, and taken to the vice president.

"Well, Sinatra saw that and said, 'I'll have one,'" Jenkins recounted. Sanders, never one to turn down a good time, had a few covert screwdrivers of his own as play continued with the gallery oblivious to the libations being shared by the vice president, Sinatra and Sanders.

"At the turn, I ask Sanders if we should get another bottle," Jenkins said. "He said, 'No, I don't think we'd be able to finish the round.'"

It would be another 10 years before a powerful man from Washington D.C., would injure a Classic spectator. This time it was Thomas P. "Tip" O'Neill, the Speaker of the House and second in line to the presidency during Ronald Reagan's White House years.

O'Neill, whose large, ruddy face, leprechaun eyes and thick shock of white hair fit perfectly in the Democratic Irish-Catholic district of Boston that he represented in Congress, had been a long-time friend of Gerald Ford. That meant Mr. Speaker and the former president joined Hope in the Classic.

O'Neill's first few years in the Classic were harmless enough. That changed in 1982, when O'Neill sent a fan to the hospital.

Playing with Ford, Hope and Bruce Lietzke, O'Neill's drive on the sixth hole of Bermuda Dunes Country Club hit the eyeglasses of Edwin Wilson, a 68-year-old fan from La Jolla, just north of San Diego. Wilson dropped immediately and doctors rushed to his side. Within 10 minutes, an ambulance was on the course, sirens wailing and lights flashing.

LEFT: Frank Sinatra, Jack Benny, Bob Hope and Vice-President Spiro Agnew holding the trophy at the 1972 tournament. *Courtesy Bob Hope Classic archives*

It wasn't until 1987 that the rotund congressman achieved lasting fame for hacker humiliation when he faced the infamous 20-foot-deep bunker on the 16th hole of the TPC Stadium Course at PGA West.

The Stadium Course was perhaps architect Pete Dye's masterpiece, drawing the quip from Hope, "It's not a golf course. It's a sentence."

O'Neill's excursion into the greenside bunker on the par-5 16th hole, dubbed by Dye the San Andreas Fault, presented him with little chance of success. If the best golfers in the world hated the course, what chance did the Boston congressman, wearing a pastel sweater and a

BELOW: Former Speaker of the House, Tip O'Neill, and President Gerald Ford in the mid-1980s.
Courtesy Desert Sun archives

ABOVE: Speaker of the House Thomas P. "Tip" O'Neill flails in vain in an attempt to get his ball out of the 20-foot-deep bunker on the 16th hole of the TPC Stadium Course at PGA West. O'Neill's efforts were highlighted on NBC's broadcast of the 1987 tournament.
Courtesy Bob Hope Classic archives

RIGHT: Former Speaker of the House, "Tip" O'Neill enjoys a relaxing moment in 1989.
Courtesy Bob Hope Classic archives

floppy hat and smoking a cigar, have?

None, as it turned out.

As America watched on TV, O'Neill's first attempt to reach the green from the bunker came up predictably short and the ball rolled back down the hill to his feet. Attempt No. 2 fared even worse, barely getting halfway up the hill before rolling back.

O'Neill's third stroke was a bit more determined, but it, too, failed to reach the top of the hill. O'Neill's

frustration got the best of him: He reached down, snatched the ball from the sand and tossed it up the hill.

The ball caught the top of the hill and began another slow descent down the slope to O'Neill's feet. The exasperated Irishman from Boston was stunned.

"We practically had to use a crane to get him out of there," Dunlevie recalled.

The Hope Tournament's ties to prominent politicians continued in 1992. That's when Dan Quayle became the

ABOVE: Representative Dan Rostenkowski reacts to his putt in the mid-1980s. Rostenkowski, chairman of the House Ways and Means Committee, was one of several politicians invited to the Classic every year.
Courtesy Bob Hope Classic archives

LEFT: President Gerald Ford, Vice President Dan Quayle and Bob Hope at Bermuda Dunes County Club during the 1992 Classic. *Courtesy Bob Hope Classic archives*

second sitting vice president to play in the tournament.

But while Quayle impressed the gallery that Saturday with a smooth, practiced swing that was the result of growing up on the fairways of Paradise Valley Country Club in Phoenix, it was Quayle's playing partner who made headlines.

John Daly had exploded onto the golf scene five months earlier with an improbable victory in the 1991 PGA Championship at Crooked Stick Golf Club in Carmel, Ind. In that short five months, Daly had developed a reputation for his awe-inspiring drives and an exaggerated backswing that would make the chiropractor of the average golfer quite wealthy.

He also was developing a reputation as the life of the

party who often spoke before he considered his words.

Daly's early rounds that week were filled with an ongoing name-calling contest with Bettye Fulford, the woman who raced out to embrace Daly on the 18th green after he won the PGA Championship. At the time, Daly announced the couple was engaged.

But by the 1992 Hope, the couple was in a heated battle, with Daly throwing barbs at Fulford from the tournament.

It was difficult to believe Fulford and Daly would eventually marry that year, especially since Daly was seen much of the tournament week at area nightspots with the three Bob Hope Chrysler Classic girls. One of the Classic girls, Paulette Dean, who wore the "Classic" shirt for the week, would eventually become Daly's third wife after he divorced Fulford.

Dean, in turn, would also divorce Daly after a notorious night of drinking in 1998 at The Players Championship in Ponte Vedra Beach, Fla. But at the 1992 Hope, Daly seemed like just another young, wide-eyed player.

"There's not many 25-year-olds who can say they played golf with Bob Hope, the vice president and a president," Daly said. "That's just such an honor. I've had a great time this week."

While the Hope Girls were part of the story in 1992 because of Daly, women were not part of the event's pro-am for more than 30 years. That changed in 1996. Amateur Mary Bell of Bermuda Dunes Country Club decided to take her husband's place in the field, becoming the first woman entered in the event.

Tournament organizers also invited basketball Hall of Famer and broadcaster Ann Meyers Drysdale to be the first woman celebrity in the field that same year, but Meyers Drysdale gave credit to Bell for breaking the gender barrier.

Breaking the gender barrier proved the Hope event was unafraid to embrace change even as a new century approached.

That was also true in the makeup of the celebrity field, where many of the great names that had been mainstays in the Hope pro-am were no longer able to withstand the rigors of the four-day event or the 18-handicap limit.

And in numerous cases, the great celebrities that ushered the Hope onto the grand stage of television had passed away.

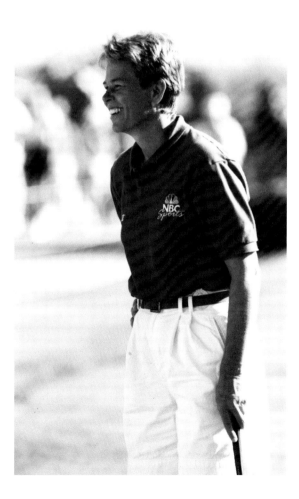

OPPOSITE: John Daly with the Hope Girls, 1992. Hope Katie Whitaker, Chrysler Danielle Marman and Classic Paulette Dean. Dean and Daly would eventually marry. *Courtesy Bob Hope Classic archives*

LEFT: Ann Meyers Drysdale in 1996. *Courtesy Bob Hope Classic archives*

Some of those attempts worked better than others. When Chicago Bears quarterback Jim McMahon played in 1988, he was a big star in the NFL. But he also played barefoot in the desert, something tournament officials frowned on. McMahon never played in the event again.

Another NFL legend, New York Giants linebacker Lawrence Taylor, also debuted in 1988. Pairing an NFL linebacker of savage intensity on the field and questionable lifestyle off the field with former President Gerald Ford initially seemed unconventional. But Taylor earned kudos from fans and was a popular addition that played in the event six more times in the 1990s.

With the popular celebrities of the day either not playing golf or tougher to get for the four days of the pro-am, tournament officials continued to turn to popular athletes. In 1996, the three great pitchers from the Atlanta Braves—Tom Glavine, John Smoltz and Greg

Maddux – played in a threesome.

The other great baseball pitcher of the decade, Roger Clemens, became a regular in the tournament. He even won the first-place crystal in the pro-am in 2006, paired with U.S. Olympic hockey star Mike Eruzione and actor and fellow Texan, Matthew McConaughey.

McConaughey represented a new generation of entertainers in the field. If the golf bug had skipped a generation of Hollywood players after Hope and the Rat

Pack, the game's popularity was starting to soar among young actors and singers in the late 1990s.

The standard bearer for the new golfer was shock rocker Alice Cooper. An admitted alcoholic, Cooper stopped drinking and filled the empty hours on the road with golf. Soon, golf replaced booze as his primary obsession and he became a fixture in golf pro-ams across the country, including the Hope.

"There was a time when I played six or seven (events) in a row," he said at the 2009 Hope. "So, I'm probably playing more golf than the pros are. I play six days a week. So everybody wants my job. I play golf in the morning and rock and roll at night. So, you can't get any better than that."

On the other end of the music spectrum was the 2002 Hope debut of singer Justin Timberlake, when he

ABOVE: WWF wrestling star Bill Goldberg, left, and golfer Peter Jacobsen congratulate each other on their good shots to the 17th green in 2002. *Courtesy Bob Hope Classic archives*

RIGHT: Roger Clemens tries to coax his ball the right way after teeing off on the 10th hole at Tamarisk Country Club during the 2005 Classic. *Courtesy Bob Hope Classic archives*

FAR RIGHT: Matthew McConaughey before teeing off to begin the first round of the Bob Hope Chrysler Classic at Bermuda Dunes Country Club, Jan. 2006. *Courtesy Bob Hope Classic archives*

OPPOSITE: Alice Cooper signs autographs after playing 18 holes at the fourth day of the Bob Hope Chrysler Classic, Jan. 24, 2009, at Palmer Private at PGA West in La Quinta. *Courtesy Bob Hope Classic archives*

was still a member of the wildly popular band N'Sync. Timberlake attracted fans to the tournament who had never stepped on a golf course before.

After the third round at Bermuda Dunes that year, Timberlake thanked the galleries by hanging around the putting green after play and signing what was estimated at about 2,000 autographs. Eventually, Timberlake would go on to serve as host of the PGA Tour event in Las Vegas.

The blend of entertainers and athletes often depended on a celebrity's work schedule. That was never truer than in 1999, when basketball greats Michael Jordan and Charles Barkley played in the field for the only time. Jordan was in the middle of one of his

retirements from the game, and Barkley played only because the NBA was in the middle of a work stoppage.

Barkley, never shy around a camera or a microphone, already earned acclaim for one of the worst golf swings ever displayed on any course. But he made news in the second round of the Hope, the day after the NBA announced labor peace.

Standing on the 10th hole at Tamarisk Country Club, Barkley signed a new contract with the Houston Rockets. Barkley's pro playing partner for the day was Daly, who joked that he was Barkley's agent on the deal.

"I only take 4 percent," Daly joked.

By the final round of the 1999 event, though, no one was talking about Barkley any more. Instead, they

OPPOSITE: Justin Timberlake, left, of the musical group, N'Sync, signs his autograph for fans after finishing Day Two of play in the 2002 Bob Hope Chrysler Classic at the Tamarisk Country Club in Rancho Mirage. *Courtesy Bob Hope Classic archives*

BELOW LEFT: A younger than usual gallery followed Justin Timberlake around Indian Wells Country Club during the 2002 Classic. *Courtesy Bob Hope Classic archives*

BELOW: Bob Hope with NBA professional basketball players Charles Barkley, left, and retired Michael Jordan, 1998. Barkley was only able to play in the tournament because of a work stoppage in the NBA. Reportedly, he negotiated his contract while playing in the tournament. *Courtesy Bob Hope Classic archives*

were talking about a bit of PGA Tour history, punctuated by ABC's Mike Tirico's words, "The best final round—EVER!"

Tirico's words from the broadcast booth were married with the image of David Duval, his shirttail hanging out of the back of his pants, pumping his fist as he danced around the 18th green of the Palmer Course at PGA West. He had just rolled in a 6-foot eagle putt to shoot a 59, 13-under par and tied for the best round in PGA Tour history.

In winning the 1999 Classic, Duval had erased a seven-shot final-round deficit with 11 birdies, six pars and the one glorious eagle on the final hole.

Duval had done more than just shoot a fabled, elusive 59. He had vaulted himself into the No. 1 spot in the world rankings, surpassing superstar-in-the-making Tiger Woods.

Duval also helped cement the Hope tournament's reputation as the PGA Tour's home for birdies, eagles and low, low scoring.

Always a tournament where players felt they could show up at the start of a season with a rusty swing and still make birdies on short courses and perfect greens, the 1990s saw remarkable feats of scoring that even Bob Hope's favorite screenwriters couldn't have conjured.

John Cook, a hometown boy who lived in Rancho Mirage just minutes from the Hope tournament office, pulled off a remarkable feat in 1992.

In a five-way playoff with O'Meara, Tom Kite, Rick Fehr and Gene Sauers, Cook played four holes in 5-under, including not one but two chip-ins. The last chip-in, an 80-footer from off the green for an eagle on the par-5 18th hole at Bermuda Dunes Country Club, denied the victory to Sauers, who played the four extra holes in four birdies and still lost.

TOP LEFT: David Duval pumps his fist as he watches his eagle putt fall on the 18th hole on the Palmer Private Course at PGA West. The eagle-3 capped Duval's record-setting 59, propelling him to the 1999 title. *Courtesy Bob Hope Classic archives*

LEFT: John Cook reacts to chipping in for a birdie on the third hole of a playoff in the 1992 Classic. The chip-in kept Cook alive in the playoff that he won with a chip-in eagle on the fourth playoff hole against Gene Sauers at Bermuda Dunes Country Club. *Courtesy Bob Hope Classic archives*

FAR LEFT: The beautiful par-5 18th hole at Bermuda Dunes Country Club has seen some of the most dramatic finishes in Classic history, including two wins by Arnold Palmer and the dramatic playoff win by John Cook in 1992. *Courtesy Bob Hope Classic archives*

OPPOSITE: John Cook accepts congratulations from Chrysler executive Steve Torok after winning the 1992 Hope while Cook's wife, Jan, and Bob Hope keep the Cook children occupied. *Courtesy Bob Hope Classic archives*

JOHN COOK

In 1993, Tom Kite flew into uncharted territory, obliterating tournament and PGA Tour scoring records with a 35-under winning total, including a 62 on the Palmer Course in the final round.

Just eight years later, Joe Durant surpassed that mark with a winning total of 36 under.

For many golf purists and some in the national media,

BELOW: Tom Kite points out his tournament-winning score of 35 under par in 1993. *Courtesy Bob Hope Classic archives*

OPPOSITE: Tom Kite is interviewed at the trophy presentation ceremony in 1993, 20 years after winning the Hope of Tomorrow championship. *Courtesy Bob Hope Classic archives*

ABOVE: Tom Kite, the 1973 Hope of Tomorrow champion, receives a kiss from Classic Queen Lynda Carter and the keys to a 1973 Maverick from Hal Barton, leasing sales manager of the Ford Division. Watching the action with Bob Hope is the previous year's tournament president and chairman, Win Fuller. *Courtesy Bob Hope Classic archives*

BELOW: Tom Kite standing next to the Ford Maverick he won for winning the 1973 Hope of Tomorrow tournament at Palm Desert County Club. Twenty years later Kite would win the Bob Hope Chrysler Classic. *Courtesy Bob Hope Classic archives*

the caliber of the Hope's winners often seemed to take a back seat to the low scoring, with winners now needing to average a birdie every third hole during the 90-hole event.

Critics couldn't help themselves from taking long-distance jabs at the desert tournament. When players angrily denounced the high rough, dried-out greens and over-par winning scores at the U.S. Open, some scribe could be counted on to joke, "What do they want this to be, the Hope?"

With a new generation of pros and celebrities coming to the tournament, Hope officials decided it might be time to revive the event's greatest tradition, the old Jam Session. But while the old Jam Session was a kind of impromptu event for tipsy participants in the 1960s and 1970s, the new party was a well-organized event.

For the 2009 event, the 50th playing of the tournament, a remarkable roster of singers and other celebrities gathered to entertain their fellow amateur players, pros and family members at the La Quinta Resort.

The evening included Huey Lewis, once kept out of the tournament because Bob Hope just didn't know about Lewis' popularity in the 1980s. Don Felder, once the guitar player of the iconic Eagles, played "Hotel California." Country singer Clay Walker ripped through a set of country and R&B hits. Michael Bolton and Josh Kelly sang a few of their hits.

And yes, Alice Cooper belted out rock anthems "School's Out" and "18."

Even first-time Hope participant Stephen Stills added a version of, "For What It's Worth," one of rock's classic anti-establishment songs that protested a world and a government of the Vietnam War era.

One had to wonder what Spiro Agnew would have thought of the changes. ∎

ABOVE: Dolores Hope takes a closer look at Joe Durant's 2001 Bob Hope Chrysler Classic Trophy.
Courtesy Bob Hope Classic archives

RIGHT: Alice Cooper (from left), Huey Lewis and Don Felder talk while on the driving range during the first day of the 50th Annual Bob Hope Chrysler Classic golf tournament at Silver Rock Resort in 2009. The three were also among the impressive roster of performers who participated in the 2009 revival of the Classic's Jam Session. *Courtesy Bob Hope Classic archives*

OPPOSITE PAGE: The 2009 Celebration Party... a new twist on the old Jam Sessions. Pictured top middle is Mrs. Arnold (Kit) Palmer dancing with John Foster, president and tournament chairman, along side Katherine Heigl, singer Josh Kelly and golf professional Bobby Clampett. Also pictured are guests enjoying the music of Michael Bolton, Kevin Nealon, Don Felder and Clay Walker.

Thanks for the memories

ABOVE: The 1996 Bob Hope Chrysler Classic Program cover featuring Bob Hope and the three presidents that played in 1995, the last hurrah for Hope as host, a position he held for more than 30 years.
Courtesy Bob Hope Classic archives

RIGHT: Fuzzy Zoeller during the 1996 Classic.
Courtesy Bob Hope Classic archives

*W*hen Bill Clinton, George H.W. Bush and Gerald Ford made history by playing together in the first round of the 1995 Bob Hope Chrysler Classic, staying with the trio shot-for-shot and step-for-step was tournament host Bob Hope. He stayed on the course for 18 holes with the presidents, even though he was 91 when that history-setting round was played.

The full round for Hope was a bit of a surprise because even before the 1995 event, he had been cutting back on his appearances. In 1992, for example, he left the first-day pairing with defending champion Corey Pavin after three holes.

The 1995 round with the presidents was basically Hope's last hurrah at his tournament. While he still made some appearances, the tournament had effectively lost its host. Hope would play a few holes at times, later cutting that down to just the occasional ceremonial shot for the gallery and television cameras.

But while Hope's age affected his play and slowed him as an amateur partner, many pros who knew Hope and his importance to the tournament and the game didn't mind.

"My last tournament was at Indian Ridge (as host course) in 1996," said former tournament director Ed Heorodt. "I put in Fuzzy Zoeller to play with Hope the last day. So I went to Fuzzy on the practice green and said, 'Fuzzy, I'm sorry I had to put you with Mr. Hope.' He said, 'That's no problem. As long as there is a Mr. Hope around, I'll be here. Put me anywhere you want.' "

Hope's cameo appearances at the tournament included teeing off during the first round Wednesday, having pictures taken with celebrities, taking a swing or two on Saturday for television and meeting the champion on Sunday.

But after Jesper Parnevik's 2000 victory at Bermuda Dunes, Hope never made another appearance at the tournament. Before the 2001 event, Dolores Hope said her husband was retired and would watch from home.

On July 27, 2003, Hope died at his Toluca Lake home – two months after his 100th birthday and five months after Mike Weir won that year's Hope title.

As the world grieved the passing of arguably the best-known entertainer of the 20th century, tributes poured in from fans, fellow entertainers, the military and politicians.

And, of course, there were tributes from the world of golf.

"In addition to his worldwide renown as an

entertainer, (Hope) was a key figure in the growth of the game of golf in America," PGA Tour Commissioner Tim Finchem said. "The tournament bearing his name, the Bob Hope Chrysler Classic, dates to 1960 and has long been one of the most successful on the PGA Tour. A mixture of great golf and entertainment, the tournament over the years has brought presidents, athletes and other celebrities together with PGA Tour professionals to raise millions of dollars for charities in the Palm Springs area."

One of the tournament's other icons lost both a

BELOW: Sweden's Jesper Parnevik, the 2000 Hope winner, signs autographs for fans in the parking lot of a course parking lot. *Courtesy Bob Hope Classic archives*

friend and a playing partner with Hope's passing.

"It was sad to get the news of Bob Hope's passing," Arnold Palmer said from his Latrobe, Pa., home. "But I think if he was here, he would want us to laugh and enjoy what he has given the world over the years."

Almost immediately and inevitably, fans asked the obvious questions: What would Hope's death mean to the tournament? How long, in fact, would it remain the Bob Hope Chrysler Classic? Would his name be removed from the tournament akin to the names of Bing Crosby and Dinah Shore being removed from their events after their deaths?

Thanks to some foresight on the part of the tournament and the Hope family, Bob Hope wouldn't be leaving the PGA Tour just yet. An agreement between the family and the tournament allows the comedian's name and ski-nose likeness to be used by the golf tournament as long as it remains a charitable tournament funding causes, such as the Eisenhower Medical Center, in the Coachella Valley.

"As far as we are concerned, it is in stone," John Foster, a member of the tournament's executive board, said just days after Hope's death. "Hope is someone who will generate emotion and admiration for as long as we

ABOVE: Dolores Hope waves to the crowd during a tribute to Bob Hope after the fourth round play of the 2004 Bob Hope Chrysler Classic. *Courtesy Desert Sun archives*

RIGHT: Former President George Bush spoke about Bob Hope from a remote location and broadcast live during a tribute to the tournament's namesake in 2004. *Courtesy Desert Sun archives*

are going to know about him. It's important for us to keep the legacy going, to be a torch bearer and annually celebrate the memory of Hope."

Another longtime pal and tournament figure saw first-hand Hope's lasting impact on people, even in the entertainer's declining years.

Eddie Susalla ran into Hope and his wife, Dolores, at Del Mar race track near San Diego, where Susalla had moved after years at Indian Wells Country Club. The Hopes and Susalla arranged for a quiet dinner in a nearby restaurant where the American icon could gaze out at the ocean.

"I asked (the restaurant) to be very quiet about it. I asked the manager for a good waiter I know, and they met us at the door and set us up at a table in the back, where there was just glass and you had all the sun (Hope) wanted," Susalla said.

"When he got up after dinner, every glass in the place went down and everyone in that place, at the bar and every table, stopped and stood up and applauded all the way from his table out to the parking lot," Susalla recalled.

"It was the damnedest thing I had ever seen. That's how popular that man was."

Even before his death, as Hope was slowly retreating from the tournament, the event itself was experiencing a kind of renaissance.

The 1980s had seen the tournament feature some relatively obscure winners, far different than the 1960s and 1970s when names like Palmer, Nicklaus, Casper and Miller were etched onto the Eisenhower Trophy.

But the winners in the 1990s and into the new century included such players as Pavin (the winner in 1987 and 1991), Tom Kite, John Cook, Scott Hoch, Fred Couples and Jesper Parnevik. They were world-class winners with major championships and Ryder Cup appearances to their credit.

And while some players stayed away from the Hope because of its five-day, four-course format or its

continued use of three amateur partners for each pro for four days, the golfers who played and succeeded found the Hope to be an early-season jump start.

"I love starting here at the Hope because it's five days of competitive golf, first of all," Phil Mickelson told reporters before teeing off in the 2004 tournament. "It's almost always perfect weather.

"Also, I got off the celebrity rotation, and when I did that, I have a quiet environment to get the year started with wonderful practice facilities," Mickelson added.

With such a positive attitude toward the tournament,

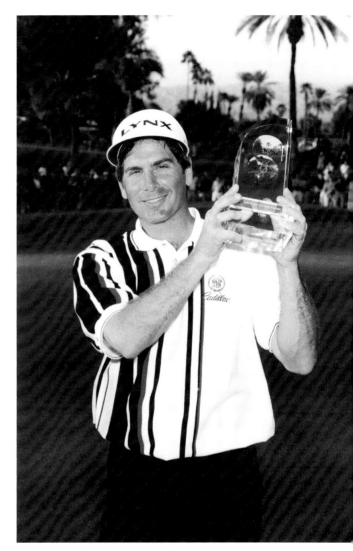

ABOVE: Fred Couples lifts Orrefors Crystal after winning the 1998 Classic at Bermuda Dunes Country Club. *Courtesy Bob Hope Classic archives*

LEFT: Corey Pavin with a clutch chip-in to beat Mark O'Meara on the first hole of the sudden death playoff in 1991. *Courtesy Bob Hope Classic archives*

it is little wonder Mickelson continued the run of strong Hope winners with victories in 2002 and 2004.

Not only did Mickelson become just the seventh player to win multiple Hope titles – reaching 30-under each time and winning in playoffs – but with Canadian Mike Weir winning in 2003, the Hope became the first PGA Tour event to be won by a lefthander in three consecutive years.

The two pulled off a stranger Hope double in 2003 and 2004, each winning the Hope and then proceeding to win the Masters later that same year at Augusta. It was a repeat of 40 years earlier, when Arnold Palmer and Jack Nicklaus won the Hope in 1962 and 1963, respectively, and then won the Masters those same years.

But the challenges the tournament faced in the new century didn't end with Hope's death. It seemed

ABOVE: Phil Mickelson checks out the Eisenhower Trophy after winning the 2002 Classic. *Courtesy Desert Sun archives*

OPPOSITE: Fans on the 18th hole of the 2002 Bob Hope Classic cheer after Mickelson wins. *Courtesy Desert Sun archives*

FAR LEFT: Mike Wier, a Canadian who won the 2003 Hope title. *Courtesy Desert Sun archives*

LEFT: Mickelson celebrates with a fist pump after sinking his put for a birdie on the 17th hole during the last day of the 2002 Classic. *Courtesy Desert Sun archives*

BELOW: Looking very confident despite the seriousness of the challenge ahead of him, Phil Mickelson makes his way toward the 18th tee tied for the tournament lead in 2004. Mickelson won, beating Skip Kendall, on the first playoff hole. *Courtesy Desert Sun archives*

like everything that had helped build the tournament in its earliest years and into the 1970s and 1980s was changing.

Palmer, the five-time winner of the tournament and still the most recognized name in the event's history, stopped playing the tournament for good in 2002.

Gerald Ford, Hope's close friend and a mainstay in the pro-am field of the event since 1977, was fighting his own battles with knee replacements and age. Like Hope before him, Ford had curtailed his appearances in the tournament to ceremonial roles, such as handing out the Eisenhower Trophy to the tournament winner.

On Dec. 26, 2006, three years after Hope's death and just 20 days before the 2007 tournament, Ford passed away at 93. The tournament had lost three of its icons: Hope and Ford to death and Palmer to age.

And even if the tournament's name was to remain the same, other aspects of the golf event, and even the PGA Tour itself, were changing. During the 1960s through the 1980s, the Hope tournament thrived on a circuit that wanted personalities to help promote professional golf. Players who might not have been crazy about the Hope's format still played because it was a chance to make a paycheck in an era when journeyman pros still struggled to make a living.

But the evolution of the tour away from celebrities and unique formats, something that had started in the 1980s, continued through the 1990s and into the new century. Companies were the new title sponsors, and corporate dollars and ever-increasing television contracts sent purses skyrocketing.

The Hope purse didn't reach $1 million until 1988. By 1998, the purse was $2.3 million, and by the time Chad Campbell won the 2006 tournament, the purse was $5 million with Campbell taking home $900,000.

The escalating money was great for players, but it also meant players could make millions of dollars while playing fewer and fewer tournaments.

The Hope began struggling to attract highly ranked players or top international stars that played few, if any West Coast PGA Tour events. It was part of a trend, led by undisputed No. 1 player Tiger Woods, that focused on building a player's schedule around major championships.

This posed challenges to board members and tournament director Michael Milthorpe, who had taken over from longtime tournament director Ed Heorodt after the 1996 tournament.

Other changes were coming to the tournament fast and furious. Most important, perhaps, were changes in the courses the Hope called home.

Starting in 1995, after PGA West in La Quinta had been sold to new owners in the fallout from the savings and loan scandals of the decade, the Hope left the Palmer Course at PGA West for Indian Ridge Country Club in Palm Desert. It was a course also designed by Palmer.

But the tournament was at Indian Ridge just three years before heading back to the PGA West complex in 1998, setting up David Duval's masterful 1999 victory.

The other Hope courses from the 1950s also found themselves under pressure.

As high-tech equipment propelled high-tech golf balls farther and farther, the older, shorter, flatter courses like Indian Wells, Tamarisk and Bermuda Dunes were yielding more and more birdies and eagles. Also, as the needs of a PGA Tour event continued to grow with hospitality tents and grandstands taking more room, the built-up private country clubs were struggling to keep pace with the space demands of the Hope event.

Eldorado left the Hope rotation after the 1989

tournament, the year Steve Jones shot a course-record 63 on the layout on the way to victory.

By the early 2000s, both Indian Wells and Bermuda Dunes were still in the tournament. However, they were no longer hosting the Sunday final round. That honor fell to the Palmer Course at PGA West, a newer course with more space for tents and galleries. Tamarisk and La Quinta country clubs remained in a two-year rotation in the tournament's four-course field.

After the 2004 tournament, tour and tournament officials announced Indian Wells would no longer be part of the field after 45 years. Tamarisk, with much less fanfare, disappeared from the four-course rotation after 2005.

To replace the older courses, Hope officials proposed sweeping changes that included two new courses: SilverRock Resort, a new Palmer-designed course developed by the city of La Quinta just one mile north of PGA West; and Classic Club, yet another course from Palmer Design, this one on the north side of Interstate 10 in the Palm Desert area 15 miles from PGA West.

Developed by the philanthropic H.N. and Frances Berger Foundation of Palm Desert as a way to raise money for its charitable efforts, Classic Club was a massive course with a layout that could stretch to 7,600 yards. It offered plenty of room for on-site parking, as

BELOW: The ninth hole at Indian Wells County Club. The lake, which separate the ninth and first holes is known as Lake Bing Phil in honor of Bing Crosby and Phil Harris, circa 1981. Indian Wells was dropped from the Classic rotation after 2004. *Courtesy Desert Sun archives*

BELOW: Caddie Bill Harmon leaps into the arms of Jay Haas after Haas won the 1988 Hope, one of the many memorable moments at Indian Wells Country Club. *Courtesy Desert Sun archives*

OPPOSITE: The Classic Club clubhouse in its final stages of completion. The building overlooked the course used in the PGA Tour event for three years. *Courtesy Desert Sun archives*

well as merchandise and hospitality tents.

The Hope and Berger Foundation agreed on a 40-year deal to play the tournament on the course, but then went an historic step further. The Berger Foundation gave Classic Club to the Hope tournament, allowing it to directly reap the benefits of proceeds from the course. The Hope became the first PGA Tour event to own its own course.

It was a good idea that quickly went wrong.

Classic Club became the most controversial course in the Hope rotation since the one-year experiment at the TPC Stadium Course at PGA West in 1987. The massive Classic Club was far different than the cozy, home-lined fairways of traditional Hope courses, leading some to say the tournament was losing its character.

More important to the professionals, Classic Club's location on the relatively undeveloped north side of Interstate 10 – which cuts through the Coachella Valley – left the course exposed to strong winds and gusts on some days. From the first year the course was played in 2006, players grumbled about the wind, the one element in golf that even pros struggle to overcome.

In 2007, the Hope had one of its worst weeks of weather in tournament history, with freezing cold and wind at all four courses. Classic Club took the brunt of the wind, including in the final round when Charley Hoffman held off John Rollins in a playoff in winds in excess of 30 mph.

When two-time Hope winner Phil Mickelson walked off the course that day and asked, "Are they going to use this course again?," the club's fate seemed sealed. After one more year, Classic Club was dropped from the rotation in favor of a second layout at PGA West, the Nicklaus Private Course.

While Classic Club felt the slings and arrows of player complaints, SilverRock Resort had a difficult journey for different reasons. The PGA Tour denied the course approval for 2006 and 2007 because of issues with flooding and erosion from unusually heavy rains

that hit the La Quinta area in 2005.

With additional work and changes in landscaping and erosion control, SilverRock finally made its debut in 2008. And while the course was another departure from the Hope's 1950s courses, it was accepted by the pros far better than Classic Club had been.

A more visible addition came to the tournament in August 2006.

Tournament officials, looking to enhance the celebrity pro-am, decided they needed a celebrity host to at least fill the role, if not the shoes, of Bob Hope. After discussing several possibilities, they turned to comedian George Lopez, who had played in the Hope before and was the star of his own hot ABC sitcom, "The George Lopez Show."

Lopez was one of the top touring comedians in the country who had done TV specials and was branching into movie work while still maintaining his popular sitcom. He also had trumpeted his love for golf, a game

ABOVE: George Lopez, left, and Craig T. Nelson entertain the crowd after finishing play for the day on the ninth green at the Indian Wells Country Club during the 2004 Bob Hope Chrysler Classic. *Courtesy Desert Sun archives*

LEFT: Comedian George Lopez poses with a cut-out of Bob Hope after making an announcement that he will be host the 48th Bob Hope Chrysler Classic golf tournament, Aug. 22, 2006. *Courtesy Desert Sun archives*

OPPOSITE: Jonathan Byrd, right, lines up a birdie putt on the ninth green at the Classic Club in Palm Desert during the first day of the Bob Hope Chrysler Classic in 2007. *Courtesy Desert Sun archives*

he said saved him from the mean streets of Los Angeles, where he had an impoverished childhood.

On Aug. 22, 2006, on the set of his show at Warner Bros. Studios in Burbank, Lopez kicked off his hosting duties by accepting the keys to a Chrysler. Immediately, he went for the laughs, promising not to sell the car for parts. Lopez understood what the Hope officials wanted him to do: Help revive lagging interest in the tournament and pump up the celebrity field through his Hollywood connections.

"When Bob was alive, the tournament was in

fantastic, fantastic shape. It generated millions and millions of dollars for charity in the desert," Lopez said on his first day on the job. "With Bob not being around, it needed a go-to guy and a voice that would carry on all of the hard work that's been done by all the people who have worked on the tournament."

It sounded promising and seemed like a logical move. But much like the move to Classic Club, bringing Lopez on as host proved to be a bit controversial. In the end, it was a short two-year experiment.

Lopez hosted in 2007 and 2008 and seemed popular

with the pros and fellow celebrities. But longtime tournament amateur players and the desert galleries seemed to have issues with Lopez, resulting in negative comments to tournament officials. There was a growing call for Lopez to not return.

What caused all the dissent? Maybe it was Lopez's desire to make the tournament more raucous and modern, while fans and amateur players wanted the tournament to revert to its past glory.

Perhaps it was a general discontent with change in the tournament, which included a new roster of golf courses.

It could be that Lopez was not a desert resident like the tournament's namesake had been. Or, perhaps it was that people around the tournament agreed that no one – not even a comedian of Lopez's popularity and stature – could or should replace Bob Hope.

In March 2008, the tournament announced Lopez would not return as host in 2009.

"We really appreciate what he has done for us. We continue to have good feelings for him," said 2008 Hope president Dave Erwin. The tournament even made a $60,000 contribution to the National Kidney Foundation in Lopez's name, as Lopez was a kidney

OPPOSITE TOP: George Lopez holds the golf ball from Charley Hoffman's eagle on the 18th hole during the Bob Hope Chrysler Classic, January 2007. *Courtesy Desert Sun archives*

OPPOSITE BOTTOM LEFT: George Lopez and Samuel L. Jackson interact with fans at the eighth tee at SilverRock Resort in 2008. *Courtesy Desert Sun archives*

OPPOSITE BOTTOM RIGHT: George Lopez dances on the first green at Bermuda Dunes after making a good shot in the first round of the 2005 Bob Hope Chrysler Classic. *Courtesy Desert Sun archives*

RIGHT: George Lopez reacts to his shot from the eighth tee at SilverRock Resort on the first day of the Bob Hope Chrysler Classic in 2008. *Courtesy Desert Sun archives*

transplant recipient.

And the winds of change raking the tournament were even blowing at Chrysler, the tournament's longtime corporate sponsor.

The auto manufacturer had been with the tournament since Hope agreed to host the tournament in the early 1960s and had taken over as title sponsor in 1985. But in the harshest economic downturn in 80 years, car makers in 2008 and 2009 were among the hardest hit.

Chrysler, now owned by a private equity firm, funded the 2009 tournament but took its name off the event, a nod to the fact it was taking billions of federal bailout dollars.

Tournament officials, while appreciative of Chrysler's long commitment to the event and the memory of Hope, had no choice but to start looking for new lead sponsor after the 2009 event.

But against the backdrop of Lopez, Classic Club and Chrysler, a familiar figure – one whose stature had been exceeded only by Hope himself – rose to host the 2009 event and the 50th playing of the tournament: Arnold Palmer.

Palmer had his own tournament at his own Bay Hill Club in Orlando, Fla., to run. But an offer to host his pal Hope's old tournament for the 50th anniversary was too tempting for him to pass up.

"I enjoyed some of my greatest success in the Hope in the early years and have loved the Palm Springs area since I first went there," Palmer said in accepting the one-year post.

"I consider it a great honor to follow in the footsteps of Bob Hope as host of this wonderful tournament, which has been a mainstay on the PGA Tour for so many years."

Palmer had not played in the event since 2002 and had been at the 2007 tournament only to announce SilverRock Resort had been cleared for the 2008 tournament. But his return as host in 2009 brought a soothing and invigorating spirit to the event.

The black-tie kick-off party seemed to have new

RIGHT: Arnold Palmer speaks to reporters during a press conference for the Bob Hope Chrysler Classic, Jan. 20, 2009, in La Quinta. *Courtesy Desert Sun archives*

energy. The galleries were buzzing with fans throughout the week. All strained to see Arnold.

It was like the return of an old friend to an appreciative neighborhood.

Players in the tournament talked about the honor of being in Hope's event, and Palmer readily defended the tournament and its format, saying he didn't accept some of the excuses some players used for not playing in it each year.

Adding to the rejuvenation of the event in 2009 was the addition of the Nicklaus Private Course at PGA West to the rotation and the return of the Palmer Course at PGA West as host.

"I think that this, the Hope tournament, needs to end here (at PGA West) on Sunday," said Pat Perez after taking the first-day lead with a 61 on the Palmer Course. "This place is phenomenal. The rotation here is awesome. It's such a good tournament as it is anyway, but I think that

OPPOSITE: A boulder juts out of a greenside bunker on the 414-yard par-4 second hole of the Jack Nicklaus Private Course at PGA West. The course was used for the 2009 Bob Hope Chrysler Classic. *Courtesy Desert Sun archives*

LEFT: Arnold Palmer laughs with Pat Perez after presenting Perez with a $918,000 check for winning the tournament on the final day of the 50th annual Bob Hope Chrysler Classic golf tournament at the Palmer Private golf course at PGA West, Jan.25, 2009. *Courtesy Desert Sun archives*

this is a great rotation and I'm just happy to be back."

Perez and others made sure another Hope tradition returned to the event in 2009 – low scoring. Perez followed his opening 61 with a 63 on the Nicklaus Private Course for a record 20-under score through 36 holes.

Through 72 holes, Perez was 30-under, but trailed Steve Stricker by three shots. As Stricker struggled on the final nine holes of a windy final round, Perez stayed steady.

On the way to his first PGA Tour victory, Perez brought back memories of David Duval, hitting his second shot on the par-5 18th on the Palmer Course to just three feet. It set up a door-slamming eagle and a 33-under winning total, tied for third-best in tournament history.

Where Perez earned his first tour victory seemed as important as how he had won it.

"I didn't get to meet Mr. Hope, but if he is anything like Mr. Palmer, then he had to be unbelievable," Perez said after the trophy ceremony. "It must have been something with Mr. Hope and Mr. Palmer and back in the day with all of their celebrity friends. I can only imagine."

The Hope had returned to its days as a festival of birdies and eagles. The 2009 event featured 12 rounds of 62 or lower, and the winning score had reached 30 under for the first time since Mickelson's second victory in 2004.

The critics and purists might roar, but the low scores had people talking about the Hope again.

In Palmer's one year as host, he had managed to revive not only memories of his reign as the king of the tournament, but also revive thoughts of his friend and tournament namesake, Bob Hope.

It was Hope, after all, who elevated the tournament's profile by becoming host in 1965.

It was Hope who brought new celebrities to the event who understood its appeal as a television show, as well as a professional golf event that embodied the marriage of sports and entertainment.

It was Hope who helped transform the tournament to a charitable powerhouse for philanthropic causes throughout the Coachella Valley. Eisenhower Medical Center and dozens of other worthwhile charities benefited from Hope's compassion and dedication to them.

And it was Hope who became an international icon through his dedication to America's soldiers and sailors. He had entertained millions through the years as a vaudevillian, a radio, television and movie star and as ambassador to hundreds of thousands of U.S. military

BELOW: Urologist Dr. John Faulkner, left, Bob Hope Chrysler Classic host Arnold Palmer, Urologist Dr. Michael Sanford, and Radiation Oncologist Dr. Paul Adams, chat about golf after Palmer announced a $250,000 for the Arnold Palmer Prostate Center at the Eisenhower Medical Center. *Courtesy Desert Sun archives*

members through U.S.O shows around the globe.

Palmer reminisced comfortably about the great days he and the game of golf had, thanks to Hope.

What ranked among his own top Hope memories? "I think the fact that Bob has always been so great and so gracious."

"Winning the tournament, having him there, was always fun for me," Palmer said. "I had opportunities to do a lot of things with Bob Hope, from playing golf to (doing a) movie, all things I thoroughly enjoyed doing

with him.

"I think probably one of the big things of his life and his career was the fact that he tied just about everything he did to his golf."

The first fabled 50 years of the Bob Hope Chrysler Classic were in the books. Even as America and the PGA Tour celebrated the milestone, officials were preparing for the next chapter in the memorable story about golf, a famed tournament and its deep roots in Southern California's desert. ∎

IT TAKES MORE THAN A GOLFER TO HAVE A GOLF TOURNAMENT . . .

100,000 Volunteers...
a lot of folks that have given their time over the years!

And those
who benefit from
everyone's efforts,

the Charities...

$47 Million

since 1960!

Index

NOTE: Page numbers in *italics* indicate a photograph on that page. Photographs on pages with text about them are not indicated with italics.